Introducing Piaget

D0145718

Jean Piaget was one of the most significant contributors to our current understanding of how children think and learn, from birth through to adolescence. In this comprehensive and accessible new book, Ann Marie Halpenny and Jan Pettersen capture the key concepts and principles of Piaget's fascinating work on children's thinking, and explore how thinking evolves and develops from infancy through the early years and beyond.

Areas covered in *Introducing Piaget* include:

- key milestones and achievements in children's thinking;
- understanding the physical world through senses and movement in infancy;
- supporting the emergence of symbolic thought and language in the early years;
- understanding object permanence;
- implications of egocentric thinking in early childhood learning and development.

Throughout the book, the consequences of these developments for children's social, emotional and intellectual development are discussed. Updates on Piaget's theory are also outlined with reference to more recent work on cognitive development in childhood. Each chapter provides a concise summary of material presented through a consideration of the implications for practice in working with children. A glossary of key Piagetian terms is also included. With a particular focus on how Piaget's principles and concepts can be applied to children in early childhood, this exciting new book is an invaluable resource for teachers, practitioners and students with an interest in learning and development in the early years.

Ann Marie Halpenny is Lecturer in Psychology and Child Development at the Dublin Institute of Technology.

Jan Pettersen is Programme Chair for the Early Childhood Education programme at the Dublin Institute of Technology.

Other titles available include

Smidt (2012) *Introducing Malaguzzi*

Loris Malaguzzi is recognised as the founder of the extraordinary programmes of preschool education that developed after the war in Reggio Emilia, Italy. In this engaging text, Sandra Smidt examines how Malaguzzi's philosophy developed out of his personal experiences of growing up in post-fascist Italy. His ideas are explored and illustrated throughout by examples relating to everyday early years practice.

Smidt (2011) *Introducing Bruner*

Sandra Smidt takes the reader on a journey through the key concepts of Jerome Bruner, a significant figure in the field of early education whose work has spanned almost a century. His wide-ranging and innovative principles of early learning and teaching are unpicked here using everyday language and the links between his ideas and those of other key thinkers of the twentieth and twenty-first centuries are revealed.

Smidt (2008) *Introducing Vygotsky*

Exploring the key concepts of Lev Vygotsky, one of the twentieth century's most influential theorists in the field of early education, *Introducing Vygotsky* emphasises the social nature of learning and examines the importance of issues such as culture, history, language and symbols in learning. This accessible text is illustrated throughout with examples drawn from real-life early years settings.

Introducing Piaget

DISCARD

A guide for practitioners and
students in early years education

Ann Marie Halpenny and
Jan Pettersen

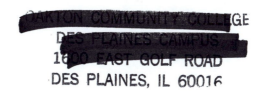
 Routledge
Taylor & Francis Group

LONDON AND NEW YORK

First published 2014
by Routledge
2 Park Square, Milton Park, Abingdon, Oxon OX14 4RN

and by Routledge
711 Third Avenue, New York, NY 10017

Routledge is an imprint of the Taylor & Francis Group, an informa business

British Library Cataloguing in Publication Data
A catalogue record for this book is available from the British Library

Library of Congress Cataloging in Publication Data
Halpenny, Ann Marie.
  Introducing Piaget : a guide for practitioners and students in early years education/Ann Marie Halpenny and Jan Pettersen.
    pages cm
  Includes bibliographical references and index.
  ISBN 978-0-415-52526-8—ISBN 978-0-415-52527-5—
  ISBN 978-0-203-11189-5   1. Education, Preschool.
  2. Piaget, Jean, 1896–1980. I. Title.
  LB1140.2.H347 2013
  372.21—dc23   2013006889

ISBN: 978-0-415-52526-8 (hbk)
ISBN: 978-0-415-52527-5 (pbk)
ISBN: 978-0-203-11189-5 (ebk)

Typeset in Galliard
by RefineCatch Limited, Bungay, Suffolk

Printed and bound in Great Britain by
CPI Group (UK) Ltd, Croydon, CR0 4YY

Contents

List of figures

Introducing Piaget

Jean Piaget was born on 9 August 1896 in Neuchâtel in the French region of Switzerland. His father Arthur was a professor of medieval literature at the University of Lausanne and also an atheist. His mother Rebecca (Jackson) was of French extraction and a devoted Christian. It appears that these conflicting religious views and beliefs were the origin of many a conflict in the Piaget household. One could only expect that these intense discussions between his parents would influence the young Jean in some way, and it is perhaps here one can find, in part, the reason why he began to develop an interest in intellectual discussion and hypothesis.

One subject matter in which he expressed an early interest was biology and he wrote his first scientific article at the tender age of 11 on the topic of the albino sparrow, an article that is widely regarded as the beginning of a quite extraordinary scientific career, in which he would go on to write several hundred articles and papers and more than 60 books. At the age of 16, Jean was offered a position as director of a museum in Geneva, an offer he kindly rejected mainly due to his age and the fact that he had not even started his third-level college studies.

Later in adolescence, he faced something of a crisis of faith and he was encouraged by his mother to attend religious instruction, but he was not convinced by the reasoning behind religious belief. Studying various philosophers and the application of logic, he dedicated himself to finding a biological explanation of knowledge, but philosophy failed to assist him in his search, leading him on to the subject of psychology.

In his work, Jean Piaget was inspired by a number of contemporary educationalists, mainly within the educational tradition to which he belongs, such as Jean Rousseau, Johann Pestalozzi, Friedrich Froebel, Maria Montessori and Célestin Freinet, in chronological order.

Rousseau (1712–1778) had argued that as the young child developed, he or she went through stages that would be characterised by the child's enhanced ability to think and process sensorial input. Further to this, Rousseau was of the opinion that all education should begin with an investigation of the child with regards to the child's particular abilities and interests, as he felt it was essential that the teacher should have this knowledge in order to provide a meaningful learning environment.

The work of Pestalozzi (1746–1827) became interesting to Piaget because he also took a strong lead from Rousseau. Piaget had been trying to implement the ideas of Rousseau in a school environment, where education would be constructed based on the child's initiative, free exploration and detailed observations. In his school, Pestalozzi introduced an understanding of how moral concepts and social interaction also could influence cognitive development. The children would participate in project work based on real-life situations, comparative to what we today see in schools with regards to project-based learning.

An essential element of Froebel's (1782–1852) concept of education is what we refer to as 'holistic learning' – the idea that education should address a wide variety of topics that develop every part of the person, physically, socially and cognitively. Although Piaget was somewhat critical of Froebel's ideas, he agreed when Froebel argued that childhood could not be viewed as a stage of preparation for the adult life, but rather as a stage in the context of lifelong learning and development.

As she studied the child, Maria Montessori discovered that the child seemed to have particular readiness for certain areas of learning at certain developmental stages. Her opinion was that, providing that the environment was a supportive one, the child would actively seek 'nourishment' for cognitive development through free exploration. This is an idea to which Piaget could subscribe, but he was rather critical of the Montessori classroom, which consists of a number of educational tools and materials, because he felt that they were self-directed and not open-ended enough to provide opportunities for the child to decide whether or not the task had been successfully carried out. Two flaws that Piaget pointed out in this scenario were the risk that the tasks did not encourage a social platform for the child to work within and also that the opportunity for creativity and exploration was severely limited.

The educationalist who perhaps was more influential on Piaget than any other was Célestin Freinet, and his educational approach is often described as a Piagetian ideal. Freinet based his approach on the innate motivation in the child to explore the environment. The child is valued as an individual in a democracy with the right to be treated as such and the teacher becomes a collaborator in the learning process, on equal standing with the child. Importantly, this also means that the child has responsibilities as well as rights. Furthermore, the school environment should present the child with elements of social life and work life. Freinet set up a print shop in his school in order to present the children with an opportunity to learn reading and writing as they engaged with the real-life process of producing printed documents for real-life customers. Piaget noted that the learning effect was obvious, because children who engaged in the project would have the drive to know how everything works, so learning evolves from simply being exposed to the process. Therefore, Freinet's learning environment meets all the requirements of 'active learning' with regards to following up on the interests of the child as well as the development of social awareness.

The work of Jean Piaget is known all over the world and is still an inspiration to practitioners and academics in fields like psychology, sociology, education, epistemology, economics and law, as witnessed in the annual catalogues of the Jean Piaget Archives. He was awarded numerous prizes and honorary degrees all over the world.

Chapter 1

Constructivism

Children as active creators of knowledge and learning

Introduction

Locating the child at the centre of their own learning is one of the most significant contributions that Piaget has made to child development. In this chapter, we elaborate on some of the key principles underpinning Piaget's constructivist approach to cognitive development in childhood. We also consider the implications of such an approach for pedagogy in early childhood. Piaget believed that children were active in constructing their development and their understanding of the environment in which that development was embedded. This perspective on learning as an individual and constructive process was in stark contrast to the passive and deterministic theories of development that had preceded it. A constructivist perspective emphasises pedagogy where action and self-directed problem-solving are viewed as being central to learning and development. Within this constructivist approach, Piaget's theory provided a focus on the progression from a concrete world in infancy, experienced exclusively through the senses and movement to a complex, abstract world in later childhood, where language and symbolic representation facilitate imagination and fantasy. In this way, the child gradually moves beyond the constraints of their own perspective and the presence of the physical environment. Significantly, the child has an active role in this progression of their thinking. Through their own actions Piaget believed the child makes sense of the world around them. Specifically, children's interactions with the physical world, and the consequences of these interactions, facilitate a more elaborate and sophisticated understanding of the world around them. This understanding increasingly relies on constructing knowledge about the world through mental representations of the environment. This evolution in the nature of thinking, and the associated increase in cognitive competence over time, is reflected in Piaget's four stages of cognitive development.

What do we mean when we use the term 'constructivism'? Lev Vygotsky (1896–1934) and Jerome Bruner (1915–) also worked within the constructivist paradigm. These three theorists share certain beliefs and understandings about how children learn, yet they differ quite clearly in certain aspects of their approaches. We will explore these differences further in chapter 2.

Constructivists are interested in the *processes* by which children construct their own knowledge (Athey, 1990). As highlighted by the author 'it could be said that constructivists are child-centred teachers who are trying to become more conscious and more theoretically aware of what is involved in the process of "coming to know"' (p. 30). When we emphasise the importance of processes and 'coming to know', it is clear that we are not focusing on outcomes in learning alone. In fact, as we will see at a later point, although Piaget was criticised for underestimating children's abilities at certain ages and stages of development – an outcome-focused approach – Piaget himself was not so interested in 'how much' children know and can think, but rather *how* children think and learn and *how* the young child's thinking processes differ from the older child's thinking processes.

Active, progressive and constructive learning

Piaget challenged traditional methods of education with a constructivist approach. Central to this approach is the concept of the child as an active learner. Activity in learning implies a dynamic process – a process which is ongoing and generates continuous change and movement in thought. As Athey expresses it, 'the life of the mind is a dynamic reality and intelligence, a real and constructive activity' (p. 33). The young child directs their own learning through an ongoing interaction with the environment around them – both in terms of the children and adults they share their time and space with, and the objects that are located in that space. The child's active role in constructing their understanding is illustrated in brief examples below.

> Bethan (5 months) reaches towards the mobile hanging over her cot, curious to touch it. After several attempts, Bethan succeeds in reaching the mobile. As she touches it, the mobile moves gently and makes a tinkling sound. Bethan stares at the mobile for a few moments and then reaches for it once more. Through her actions and experiences with the external world, Bethan's reality now expands to incorporate objects that move and objects that make a sound when they move.

Margaret Donaldson (1978) has shown how hard children work to bring their previous experience to bear on new situations and how important it is for children to consolidate their new learning in situations that allow this. Donaldson and others have shown how young children, exposed at too early

Lewis (3 years, 5 months), playing with water in the water area in his crèche, realises that water splashes outwards, can be used to fill and empty containers, feels wet on his skin and clothes, can be poured from one object to another. Lewis' awareness of the properties and principles of liquid is expanding through his activities and experiments with water. He is realising that when he pours water through a funnel it drops in a particular way – in a skinny, almost straight line.

an age to formal, decontextualised learning, may learn failure. Donaldson argues powerfully that young children, in order to be able to build on what they already know and can do, need to be in situations that make 'human sense' to them.

We can see the pattern emerge of an ongoing process of experience, reflection on that experience and continuous updating of mental representations of the world in order to make that representation more accurate. This pattern of learning can be compared to the movement of a spiral – continuous, dynamic experience gathering new information that allows learning to expand, move to a more sophisticated level and reflect more precisely the properties and mechanisms of the world around the child.

To summarise, children construct a mental image of the world through experience, and by means of continuous updating, they align that mental image further and more precisely with the reality of the world around them. We can compare this process to updating the technologies with which we are working on a daily basis – our computers, smartphones, etc. – all require updating on a regular basis. This ongoing process of updating and re-aligning mental representations (similar to a computer) is the key mechanism through which children construct their mental worlds and through which they play an active, central role in the learning that follows this process. We think of Piaget's constructivist pedagogy, therefore, as being *active*, *progressive* and *constructive*.

- Active ⇒ child is self-motivated to explore the environment and to interact with it and the pace of learning is regulated through the child's actions.
- Progressive ⇒ child is becoming more competent over time at carrying out actions and interactions on the environment, and the complexity of these actions is, in turn, steadily increasing over time.
- Constructive ⇒ progression is dependent on building up more sophisticated mental representations as a result of experiences and actions located in the external world.

Charlie (4 years, 5 months) loves dinosaurs. When it's time to choose an activity in his preschool, Charlie often likes to read books about dinosaurs. At first he spent his time looking at the illustrations and naming some of the different dinosaurs with his key worker. He later began to match the plastic figures that represented the different dinosaur types depicted in the books. Through his interest in dinosaurs and his activities looking at the books, his understanding changed from one where all dinosaurs were the same to one where there were many specific types of dinosaurs and each of these types had a particular name and appearance.

Charlie's learning is, first of all, motivated by his interest in dinosaurs, which spurs him on to activities related to finding out more about dinosaurs. Through his actions he gradually constructs a new and more complex understanding of dinosaurs.

Looking back to previous theories

The constructivist perspective on learning as an active, progressive and constructive process was in stark contrast to the more passive and deterministic theories of development that had gone before. The sections below briefly review some of the key principles of these earlier theories.

Behaviourism

One of the most influential theories to shape our knowledge about child development was behaviourism, which took hold as a very dominant school of thought around the beginning of the 20th century. Theorists such as John Watson (1878–1958) and B. F. Skinner (1904–1990) had put forward the view that all humans are born *tabula rasa* (blank slates). In other words, we are all born the same and everything we become depends on how the environment shapes us. Two behavioural concepts – reinforcement/reward and punishment – were highlighted as key principles in beliefs about child-rearing strategies. For the behaviourists, reinforcement was rewarding certain behaviours in order to ensure that they are maintained and increased. So, the principles of praising and rewarding children with treats for good behaviour and punishing children for bad behaviours largely developed from the behaviourist perspective and these principles dominated child-rearing practices for much of the 20th century. In the middle of the 20th century, behaviourism was further updated to allow for a less passive portrait of development in social learning theory approaches. Unlike the early behaviourists, Albert Bandura (1925–) placed great emphasis on children observing the world around them, and cognitively selecting which modelled behaviours to imitate.

> Lorraine (early years practitioner) has explained to a small group of toddlers that lunch is about to be served and has requested that everyone sits down at the table while they are waiting for lunch to be served. Leah (2 years, 8 months) begins to tap her spoon on the side of the table, making a noise, which attracts the attention of several children nearby. Paul (3 years) giggles in amusement at the sound and begins to imitate Leah's actions.

Paul's imitation of Leah's actions above provides a very simple example of one of the principles of social learning theory – children observe and imitate select behaviours modelled by other people in their environment.

Critical reflection

Behaviourist principles suggested that children, and people in general, could be controlled and shaped in a way that greatly undermined the child's individual motivation and agency in actively learning and developing. To some extent, children were viewed as being uninvolved in their own development and having little or no role to play in their learning and development. So, one of the main criticisms of this approach was that it tended to conceptualise learning as passive and controlled.

Psychoanalysis

Another very influential theory to shape our understanding of child development and learning was the psychoanalytical perspective. Briefly, psychoanalysis placed a lot of emphasis on social and emotional development. Sigmund Freud (1856–1939) developed this theory, which outlined key features in human development across the lifespan. At birth, Freud maintained that the mind largely consisted of primitive drives and instincts, which were called the *id*. During early childhood, the *ego* or self emerges. With this added dimension to the social and emotional world of the young child, they are able to regulate to a greater extent the primitive instincts of the *id*.

> Ruby (3 years, 4 months) is in the outdoor area of her day-care setting. She is finding it hard to focus on the activities around her, but is following intently the movements of Simon, who has been driving

around in the truck mobile for the last 10 minutes. Ruby wants to drive the truck mobile but Janet, her key worker, has explained several times that Ruby must wait until Simon has finished playing with it. When Simon has finished, Ruby's turn will come.

So Ruby, although distressed at the idea that somebody else is playing with the truck nonetheless can accept that if she waits her turn, she too can play with this toy. Ruby has developed the ability to delay gratification of impulses in order to meet society's demands, particularly the demands conveyed by parents and caregivers.

Critical reflection

Psychoanalysis has been criticised because of its over-emphasis on physical and sexual drives in humans. Much of Freud's theory was derived from observations on a very small number of children. While psychoanalysis has been useful in helping us understand the emotional influences on a young child's life and the importance of emotional experiences during the early years, the active role of the child in their learning and development does not figure very strongly in such a theory.

From concrete to symbolic experience and understanding

In contrast with these older theories, Piaget's constructivist perspective emphasises pedagogy where action and self-directed problem-solving are viewed as being central to learning and development. Such a pedagogy also emphasises progression from a physical, concrete world in infancy, experienced exclusively through the senses and movement to a complex, abstract world in later childhood, where language and symbolic representation facilitate imagination and fantasy.

Let's think a little about how this progression from an exclusively physical, sensory world to a world of images evolves. We will look more precisely at this within each of the chapters that deal with Piaget's four stages of cognitive development. The very young infant's life is dominated to a great extent by biological and physical needs – sleep, food and warmth (Smidt, 2011). However, as children grow they become less dependent on a physical world exclusively and begin to move into a world that also includes listening, looking, feeling, experiencing and thinking. While Vygotsky saw this move from physical needs to higher mental functions as being mediated by adults or more experienced and expert peers, Piaget did not emphasise the adult input and saw the child's learning as being largely self-directed. For Piaget, the child was *a little scientist*, exploring and reflecting on these explorations to increase competence. Vygotsky is described as a *social constructivist* – in other words, he shared Piaget's belief that children actively construct their own learning and development. In contrast to Piaget, however, Vygotsky saw the adult as intervening and aiding this learning and the social and cultural context was centrally highlighted.

The child gradually moves beyond the constraints of their own perspective and the presence of the physical environment. Importantly, the child plays an active role in this progression of their own thinking. The cognitive journey from sensorimotor actions in infancy to abstract thought in late childhood and early adolescence is captured by Miller:

> Through millions of transactions with the environment and reflections on these transactions, children move from an understanding of the world based on action schemes, to one based on representations, to one based on internalised, organised operations. The beauty of this is that it is orderly.
>
> (2011, p. 165)

Let's try to take a closer look at what is meant when we talk about moving from the physical, concrete world to a more symbolic and ultimately abstract representation of the world around us. As Athey points out:

> Many skills begin with sensorimotor action although internalisation of action is speeded up by verbal (symbolic) instruction. During its first months, a child has certain elementary motor behaviours such as sucking, banging, looking, smelling and waving and so on. Each of these behaviours when applied to objects brings sensory feedback.
>
> (1990, p. 34)

So to summarise, sensorimotor actions such as banging on a hard object like a table or chair generates the sensory feedback that banging on hard objects makes a particular loud sound, while banging on something soft such as a cushion or a soft toy makes very little sound or no sound at all. Central to the constructivist view of learning is this understanding of the relationship between the motor actions of the child and the sensory or perceptual feedback that follows.

Knowledge and the world are both constructed and constantly reconstructed through personal experience (Ackermann, 1996). Piaget's constructivism offers us a window into what children are interested in and able to achieve at different stages of their development. The theory describes how children's ways of doing and thinking evolve over time and under which circumstances children are more likely to 'let go of – or hold onto – their currently held views' (Ackermann, 1996, np).

Banging on table with a metal spoon **Motor action**		Banging hard object with hard object makes a loud sound **Sensory feedback**

Figure 1.1. Sensorimotor learning

The child's construction of the world is further mediated, supported and enabled with the emergence of language. Language provides children with an additional dimension to their experiences and a means of translating the sensory feedback received from sensorimotor action and recording it internally or *internalising it*. At this new stage of symbolic functioning, it is not just the relationship between motor action and effects that generates information. For example, the sensorimotor infant is dependent on seeing and experiencing effects in the physical world in order to understand how things work. A young child may fit together 10 hollow blocks in a size series. The sensorimotor child will have little or no knowledge of size seriation and so may need to repeat the fitting actions of one block inside another 30 or 40 times in order to succeed (Athey, 1990). Once the child is able to represent the effects of an experience in symbols or language, they can internalise or store the feedback as a 'rule' or 'operation' and this speeds up learning and makes it more efficient. A big block does not fit into a smaller block and this becomes a guiding principle that allows the child to avoid making such an error in future actions. With each of these new guiding principles the world is transformed and reconstructed once again.

So to summarise so far some of the features of Piaget's constructivist theory:

- Children construct knowledge about the world around them through their actions.
- Learning begins with physical actions and is informed by the sensory feedback that is generated by these actions and that produces effects.

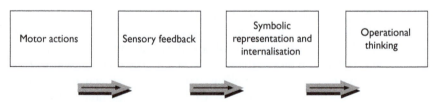

Figure 1.2. From motor actions to operational thinking

- Children's thinking is enhanced by symbolic representations mainly through language, which allows them to internalise these *effects* and translate them into principles/rules/operations.
- Operational thinking takes place when the child moves beyond an understanding of the relationship of action to effect and knows that there is an unchanging correspondence between certain kinds of actions (operations) and certain kinds of effects (transformations).
- Knowledge about the world is constructed progressively over time and becomes more complex as feedback is provided and processed from the external world.
- The construction of knowledge can be likened to a spiral movement, where in tandem with the child's continuous experience, thinking and understanding expand and allow a more accurate picture of the world and its mechanisms to be recorded.

Key concepts in constructivist pedagogy

1. *Discovery learning:* one of the greatest contributions that Piaget's constructivist theory has made to the field of early childhood, and child development more broadly, is the notion that the child develops a more abstract and general capacity to tackle problems in the world in a very independent way (Oates *et al.*, 2005). In contrast to Vygotsky, who emphasised learning with the assistance of adults, Piaget's theory supports the pedagogic principles of discovery learning, where a rich learning environment is the predominant feature and where direct tuition is not emphasised. Generating opportunities for active exploration and investigation of concepts and physical events is central to such an approach so that children can construct and understand based on their experiences. An interesting feature of Piaget's approach is that although he did not foreground the adult role in supporting children's learning, he valued peer contact as a means through which the child could be exposed to conflicting viewpoints in a way that would prompt them to engage in thoughtful evaluation of the ideas being presented.

2. *Active learning:* discovery learning by its name implies activity in the learning experience. The process of learning consists of an active construction of knowledge. The teacher, therefore, must arrange things so that knowledge is actively constructed and not simply copied or transmitted.

3. *Children at the centre of learning:* constructivist pedagogy places the child at the centre of their own learning. Teachers and practitioners are encouraged to be mindful of what the child is bringing to the learning situation as well as what they, as teachers, might wish to transmit. Constructivists arrange learning environments in such a way that the

child and the teacher negotiate and make meanings together (Athey, 1990).

4. *Observing children:* one of the great strengths of Piaget's theory is that he developed his approach to learning based on very detailed, practical, precise and attentive observation of young children – mostly his own children, Laurent, Lucienne and Jacqueline. Paying attention to the detail of children's interests and abilities, noting their changing competences, their movement to more complex thinking patterns, and individual differences in development are central elements in constructivist pedagogy. Through observations and reflective practice, practitioners working with children in the early years document and accumulate a deep understanding of children's changing patterns in cognition and related aspects of the child's development.

5. *Theory informed through practice:* Piaget's constructivist theory emphasised that action comes before knowledge and, therefore, theory can only be informed by action in practice. A number of approaches to early childhood education are aligned to such an approach. For example, approaches such as HighScope, Reggio Emilia and Froebel foreground playful, active engagement in real-life experiences using real materials.

Chapter 2

The landscape of cognitive development in childhood

Introduction

Cognitive development refers to the changes and growth in thinking processes such as memory, problem solving and reasoning. This chapter aims to provide a simple overview of the domain of cognitive development in childhood. While exploring this aspect of development, we will also try to draw in some of the implications of cognitive development for other aspects of development such as social and emotional knowledge. Links between play and cognitive development are also considered. We will conclude this chapter with some reflections on Piaget's stage theory of cognitive development, the implications of this stage theory for early childhood education and, finally, draw together information on some of the key theorists who were working in the field of cognitive development both at the time of Piaget and since then.

Defining cognitive development

Cognitive development refers to knowing, understanding, mental representation, thinking and remembering and how these processes change and develop as children grow through infancy and early childhood. As Schaffer expresses it:

> Included here are processes such as perception, remembering, classifying, understanding, reasoning, thinking, problem-solving, conceptualising, classifying and planning – in short, all those expressions of human intelligence that we use to adapt and make sense of the world.
>
> (2006, p. 96)

Meaning making

One of the greatest challenges in early childhood is making meaning of all the novel experiences that arise on a daily basis. Smidt (2011) draws attention to the many ways in which children work hard to make sense of the world, in particular with regard to learning to interpret the signs and symbols in their environment. Vygotsky and Bruner highlighted the central role that language plays in this process of making sense or making meaning of our experiences.

Andrew (2 years) likes playing in the home corner, which has been set up as a shop, with empty boxes, tins and other items that you may find in a store. Andrew likes to hold the items, explore colours, images, weight and property. At this age, children increase their understanding of object names and Andrew is repeating words that he knows throughout the activity and his key worker is repeating the words back to him to reinforce his experience and also correct pronunciation. He has been to the shop with his mother and knows that she puts shopping items into the trolley, so he is mimicking her actions using a play-size trolley.

Andrew (now age 4) is playing shop with a group of children in the home corner. He is carrying a bag that has the function of a shopping basket. He picks items from the shelves and puts them into the basket. Placing the items in the bag requires both dexterity and concentration, and as he walks around the 'shop', he negotiates price and quality of the items with the other children who work in the shop. Andrew really enjoys the activity and he likes exploring his role as a customer and relates it to that of the shopkeeper. This play activity will allow Andrew to understand the issues as an active agent in the process, not just as an observer.

Curiosity is one of the main driving forces of children's search for meaning, while having a sense of agency, or belief in having some control over the learning process, is also central to cognitive development (May, 2011). Piaget also drew attention to children's self-motivation to act on and explore their environments while Bruner (1976) emphasises learning experiences which are anchored in a concrete situation and therefore more meaningful and purposeful for the child. Knowledge that is not linked to a particular experience or event may be detached and therefore less meaningful and accessible to the child. Concrete, first-hand experiences, on the other hand, allow children to access knowledge about the world, which, in turn, helps them to make sense of their own experiences.

Let's explore what cognitive development can mean in action through a focus on children's activities in infancy and early childhood as presented in the following example.

Rachel (7 months) sits in her high-chair while her mother prepares her food. A toy car, a little colourful clown and some crayons are on her tray. Rachel picks each one up and explores them by putting them into her mouth, pushing them up and down the tray and finally pushing them off the tray on to the floor where they make a crashing sound as they reach the ground. Her older brother Jake (5 years), who is playing nearby, picks up the toys and puts them back on the tray. Rachel, delighted at her ability to 'make things happen' in the world around her, once again pushes the objects off the tray to land on the floor. This time Jake is not pleased and complains to his mother that Rachel is annoying him.

Rachel and her brother Jake are obviously at different stages of development and we can see these differences in action with regard to their cognitive processing and understanding of the same event – Rachel's pushing objects off her tray. The discovery that she can make objects fall to the ground provides Rachel with feelings of mastery and consequent delight, which motivate her to repeat her actions again and again. However, Jake has moved into a different stage of cognitive development where he is no longer dependent on the sensorimotor world alone to inform his actions. For him, Rachel's actions seem futile, with no particular purpose other than to annoy him. Much of Rachel's learning and development is supported through what Piaget termed sensorimotor activity. In other words, her understanding of objects and their properties is very dependent on her ability to see, hear, touch, taste and feel the objects around her. As highlighted by DeHart *et al.* (2004), language and abstract concepts are not yet evidently part of her thinking. What she knows and remembers is directly tied to what she can see, hear, feel, taste, touch and do.

Jake, on the other hand, uses language to express his annoyance and irritation at Rachel's actions. Jake is able to *think* about things even when they are not physically present. He has developed what is termed 'mental representation' – the ability to store images and symbols in memory. As they move through early childhood, children begin to understand the world at an ever more advanced level, putting emphasis on *how* things work and *why* events take place. While the discovery for Rachel that she can 'make things happen' in the world allows her a great sense of delight and achievement, Jake interprets her actions in a very different way – seeing them as unnecessary and pointless and causing annoyance and irritation through their disturbance of his own play activities.

One of the important differences in the abilities of Rachel and Jake is their ability to *read* and cognitively *process or interpret* the information in the environment around them. So, cognitive abilities are not simply focusing on intellectual activity but are closely tied in to children's social behaviours and the ability to read and interpret the feelings and intentions of others. In later chapters, we will look in more detail at the precise changes and advances in cognitive development that take place as children move through infancy to toddlerhood and preschool cognitive abilities. As emphasised in the previous chapter and illustrated in the examples of Rachel and Jake above, children are active participants in their cognitive development. Infants explore, examine and manipulate novel objects that come their way. Through their explorations and interactions with objects and people in their environment and the associated feedback from these actions, their cognitive abilities develop and progress to allow more intentional planning of activities and a more complex understanding of the possible consequences of actions.

Play and cognitive development

Piaget was very interested in play and its relationship to cognitive development and defined play as 'a process of assimilation of experiences through which a child reaches higher levels of cognitive development' (Piaget, 1951, p. 87). In fact both Piaget and Vygotsky emphasised the importance role play had in facilitating an understanding of daily events and believed play to be a source of creative imagination, although as we will see later, Piaget emphasised that play served more as an index of the child's ability rather than promoting cognitive development.

As we move through this book, we will see Piaget's theory applied to practice in the early years. One illustration of this is what has been termed 'schematic play' (May, 2011, p. 24), where children are supported in practising a new concept by repeating it in a playful context over and over again until that concept is established and anchored in their minds.

At the age of 3, Marcus spent all his time playing with his Matchbox cars. He owned a whole carrier bag full of them and he would spend long stretches of the day organising the cars in a long row as in a traffic jam, or side by side like a car park. One day, completely out of the blue, Marcus collects sheets of paper and a roll of sticky tape and starts wrapping up each car very carefully, each in one sheet of paper. Over the following days, he continues this operation, until all cars have been wrapped. He then proceeds to put them into the carrier bag, which he places in his bedroom closet. Marcus's behaviour is building on an enveloping schema, where the child has a desire to cover up, or wrap up things. Building on Piaget's schema theory, Chris Athey (1990) described schema as 'patterns of behaviour' that allow the child to explore a particular concept, such as height, weight, velocity, volume, capacity etc. Staff at the world-famous Pen Green Centre have identified 36 different schemas, but there are probably more.

Spontaneity is a key feature of children's play and it is this feature that allows children the freedom to explore and to make connections between familiar and novel information. One of the earliest sources of creative imagination is the ability of the child to substitute one object for another in pretend play.

> Pretend play requires the ability to transform objects and actions symbolically; it is furthered by interactive social dialogue and negotiation; and it involves role taking, script knowledge, and improvisation.
>
> (Bergen, 2002, np)

Pretend play, which children experience as a simple, natural and enjoyable activity, nonetheless involves a number of complex skills, as we can see from this definition. Piaget (1951) saw pretend play as an indication of the development of symbolic representation – the ability to separate an idea from its referent or something that represented it. However, as mentioned previously, Piaget did not make strong claims for the promotion of cognitive development through play (Lillard *et al.*, 2012).

Vygotsky (1967), on the other hand, believed that children develop their ability to symbolically represent objects through pretend play and posited a causal link between play and cognitive development. More recently, studies have drawn attention to the benefits for children's cognitive skills of their involvement in pretend play. For example, long-term capacities related to metacognition (the ability to think about your own thinking), problem solving and social cognition through engagement with pretend play have been identified (Bergen, 2002). The author goes on to specify that complex and multidimensional skills involving many areas of the brain are most likely to flourish in environments where there are opportunities for high-quality pretend play. If we pause for a moment to reflect on the following extract from *The Power of Play* (Brennan, 2004), it becomes clearer how these abilities may well be supported through pretend play.

> The children are very involved in role play. At times, they step outside it to plan and decide on the appropriate script for each person. The boys are describing to their teacher, Siobhan, what they have to do. The fire brigade is on an emergency mission and both boys grab the steering wheel and take off. One of them collapses and plays dead, while the other resuscitates him. An instant recovery allows them both to move on, always under terrible pressure, to face the next challenge. There's a problem with the baby, he must be taken to hospital immediately. With three more passengers on board, they negotiate traffic, sharp bends, traffic lights and all the hazards and noises of the journey are reflected in the commentary of the drivers. Then lo and behold, another accident

occurs. Now all the passengers are spread out on the ground and the driver is calling emergency services.

(Brennan, 2004, p. 4)

In a review of the evidence on the impact of pretend play on children's development, Lillard *et al.* (2012) conclude that the Piagetian notion that pretend play can be seen as an *index* of cognitive function (rather than a promoter of cognitive function) may be supported. In this recent review, the evidence for a causal link between play and cognitive outcomes is not supported. Significantly though, the authors clarify that 'playful learning' (Hirsh-Pasek *et al.*, 2009), which is child-centred and involves intrinsically motivated learning opportunities and peer interaction, is the most positive learning method for children's development.

Practitioners' perspectives on children's thinking in the early years

When we talk about 'thinking', we are talking about something that involves much more than just the acquisition of knowledge, as highlighted by Robson and Hargreaves (2005), who go on to specify that critical judgement, creativity, decision making, and the ability to act independently and to reflect on one's own thinking (metacognition) are all part of what we tend to call 'thinking'. Setting the context and rationale for a small qualitative study carried out with five early years practitioners which explored their views on the development of thinking in children aged 3–5 years, Robson and Hargreaves (2005) point out that it is only relatively recently that more emphasis is being placed on children's thinking in the early years and how teachers and practitioners can support these activities. Previously, the emphasis had been exclusively on thinking in older children (Wallace, 2002). One interesting finding that emerged from this small study was that supporting the development of young children's thinking is not always an explicit part of planning in early years settings. Findings also highlighted the importance of placing an emphasis on the child's own choices, sufficient time to carry out child-chosen activities, and opportunities for talking and communicating with children for practitioners to be able to better support thinking in the early years. The limitation of conceptualising 'thinking' narrowly as a problem-solving activity emerged in the views of the practitioners. Moreover, the potential benefits of providing a greater emphasis on other aspects of thinking such as children's conceptual development, imagination and creativity (Thornton, 2002; White, 2002) were also outlined and discussed. Making connections between knowledge that has already been acquired and something new is central to cognitive development (May, 2011) and this is most likely to occur when resources are rich in terms of their potential for creative thinking in an effort to forge the relationship between knowing and feeling.

How is cognitive development linked to other aspects of development in childhood and beyond?

According to Meadows:

> Virtually every human action involves some thinking, learning, use of concepts and so forth and is, therefore, cognitive. The problem with talking about separate domains of development is that it underplays the links between these different domains – as for example the links between cognition, emotion, social knowledge.
>
> (1993, p. 2)

What Meadows draws attention to in this quote is the artificial separation that psychologists tend to create between different aspects of our development, such as cognitive, emotional and social development. In focusing specifically on cognitive development in childhood, it can be argued that Piaget did not emphasise the importance of such development for children's emotional and social worlds. This link between how we perceive, interpret and ultimately understand the world around us and how this understanding, in turn, affects how we feel about what happens to us can help us as educators better understand children's development in different domains. For example, a focus on how children's thinking develops in their first years of life allows us to gain insight into specific aspects of their development such as children's awareness of themselves as separate entities, changes in egocentric thinking, the development of emotional regulation, empathy and perspective taking and the activities that are associated with supporting these aspects of development.

Social cognition

Social cognition refers to cognitive abilities that are more specifically involved in social interaction. For example, the ability to understand intentions, to negotiate and share, to take the perspective of another person – these abilities are rooted in cognitive development and, as we can see, they are essential to communicating and getting on with others around us. In order to understand ourselves and other people, we need to develop an understanding of emotions, and this is an ability that increases through infancy and early childhood.

The cognitive ability to read emotions and understand how these emotions are often expressed in terms of postures, movement and facial expressions and tones of voice are all essential skills we develop that help us to better understand, predict and control actions in the world around us. Meadows (1993) emphasises the need for children to learn the skills to cooperate and to compete with one another. We will return to this topic in later sections of the book and find out more about research that has been carried out on children's ability to understand the perspectives of others – much of which has been carried out under the broad term 'theory of mind' abilities. Specifically, theory of mind abilities involve being able to infer the full range of mental states (beliefs, desires, intentions, imagination, emotions, etc.) that cause action (Baron-Cohen, 2001). Difficulty in understanding other minds is a core cognitive feature of autism spectrum conditions.

A final word on how cognitive development goes far beyond the ability to think and process information merits acknowledgement of how cognitive development and the theories associated with this area have contributed to the development of effective treatments and therapies. One very helpful illustration of such an influence on therapy is cognitive behavioural therapy (CBT), which draws together principles from both the behavioural and cognitive schools of psychology. The cognitive component of such a therapy focuses on deficiencies and/or distortions in the way in which an individual may be processing or interpreting information and works with the individual to try to illuminate these and to replace such processing with more accurate reading of events and others' intentions.

Piaget's stages of cognitive development

Piaget's legacy is perhaps most often acknowledged with reference to his identification of 'structurally different, pre-operational and operational, structures of the mind' (Wood, 1998, p. 59). Putting this into simpler language, Piaget made it possible to consider planning for children's learning and development based on the concept of *universal* periods or stages in children's lives, during which thinking shares key features of all children's thinking within this age range, and, conversely, periods of time that are qualitatively different in terms of the associated thinking structures related to children's age. Piaget put forward a theory that involved four distinct stages of cognitive development and we will highlight these stages and the abilities associated with each stage in chapter 3. While Piaget himself did not specify the implications of his theory for education at any age, his ideas, in particular of specifying the sequence in which children learn certain concepts, were soon adopted to build a new theory of learning readiness that allowed teachers and practitioners to align their approaches to teaching and teaching methods with the cognitive level of the children they were teaching.

Yet, it is this very feature of Piaget's theory that has most often been the target of critical comment and challenge. Working closely with young children, we know that abilities and competencies, while broadly following a stage-like sequence, emerge in many and differing ways among young children. Some of the areas that have been transcended since Piaget's theory include:

- The view that there is a unified system of general intelligence that shifts according to a child's age alone has been largely rejected in favour of a modular system, where children do not acquire concepts and broad conceptual structures across all content areas as Piaget suggested (Miller, 2011).

- Stage-based approaches to education in the early years have been rejected due to the prescriptive nature of the learning environment that might be generated by such an emphasis on age and developmental stage.
- Each child's development and progress is strongly influenced by the particular constellation of factors that makes up the context in which their development is occurring. Piaget's theory of cognitive development is invaluable in pointing up developmental milestones achieved by most children, at particular stages in their development. However, the complexity of each individual child cannot be captured in developmental stages alone.
- Current models of early childhood education, such as Reggio Emilia, are built around the notion that human interaction and the physical and cultural environments in which learning takes place are central to any educational approach.

Broadly, we know that Piaget's theory tended to underestimate some aspects of cognitive ability in childhood and neglected to include reference to the social and cultural contexts in which learning is occurring. However, despite these limitations and acknowledging that Piaget overestimated the role of logic in intellectual development, Wood (1998) states that there are many contemporary theorists who suggest that there are discontinuities in children's cognitive development and that thinking does indeed change with age. We will return to a more detailed conversation on the merits and demerits of Piaget's stage theory of cognitive development in later chapters.

The landscape of cognitive development since Piaget

Before we consider the theories that have developed following Piaget, we will look briefly at two very well-known psychologists who also worked on theories of cognitive development in childhood and whose theories have also been very influential in education. Below we highlight briefly some of the similarities and differences that characterise these theorists.

Lev Vygotsky (1896–1934)

Lev Vygotsky was a Soviet psychologist who, during his relatively short life, managed to influence considerably psychological thinking and education. Similar to Piaget, Vygotsky focused on thinking and cognitive development in childhood. Much of Vygotsky's theory emphasised the importance of language in learning and development. Both Piaget and Vygotsky were

constructivists – they posited theories where children were active con-
structors in their own knowledge and development. Piaget and Vygotsky
differed most significantly in the emphasis that Vygotsky placed on socio-
cultural influences on development. Vygotsky was a social constructivist
because his theory of cognitive development highlighted the important role
that adults and more expert peers can play in helping children learn. Social
constructivism puts forward the view that knowledge is constructed through
an understanding of social and cultural interactions and by the collaborative
nature of learning. Instruction was a term that was foregrounded in Vygotsky's
theory and language was one of the major tools used in this instruction.
Some of the concepts that have been developed by Vygotsky and adopted by
early childhood practitioners include:

Internalisation: Children learn through a process of internalisation.
    This refers to the merging of language and thought that facilitates
    reasoning.
Scaffolding: Supporting and promoting learning through appropriate guid-
    ance, which is carefully tailored and adjusted to the changing needs of
    the child's developmental level.
Zone of proximal development: The difference between what a child can
    achieve alone and what they can achieve with the help and support of
    others.

Jerome Bruner (1915–)

Jerome Bruner is an American psychologist whose theories have also exerted
a significant influence on developmental psychology and education. Similar
to Piaget and Vygotsky, Bruner emphasises the importance and central role
of action and problem solving in learning and development. The benefits of
establishing deep connections between activities involved in the solution of
practical concrete problems and more abstract processes were highlighted by
both Piaget and Bruner. Children will only understand and be able to generalise information about abstract concepts if these are grounded in practical
problem solving. Bruner also emphasised stages in his theory of development
but he did not suggest that these stages represented different *modes of thought*
at different times during development, as Piaget did. For Bruner, progression
through these stages involved a gradual development of cognitive skills that
evolved in a smooth progression towards more sophisticated cognitive tech-
niques. In contrast to Piaget, Bruner did not support the notion of readiness
for learning and felt that this approach was limiting in that it held children
back from more advanced learning.

A number of other developments within cognitive psychology, strongly
influenced by Piaget's theory of cognitive development, are very briefly
summarised below.

Information-processing models of cognitive development provided the main theoretical alternative to Piagetian and Vygotskian modes of cognitive development (Halford and Andrews, 2011). A key influence on cognitive psychology in the second half of the twentieth century was the development of computers. Information processing as a model of how human thought works studied processes such as storing and retrieving information in order to better understand how cognitive development proceeds. As described by Goswami:

> The child takes certain input, converts them into representations, and then uses these representations to compute certain outputs.
>
> (2011, p. 643)

The goal of these theories was to attempt to explain data collected by Piaget and those working within a Piagetian framework. Information processing abilities such as memory capacity and the ability to coordinate different inputs were analysed against this framework.

Theory of mind refers to the ability of an individual to attribute mental states to other people. In other words, the ability of the child to understand that other people have beliefs, intentions and desires that may not correspond to their own. Piaget's view that related concepts are interdependent and form a coherent cognitive system influenced the development of theorists working within this field of cognitive psychology (Miller, 2011). One of the concepts that Piaget drew attention to within his theory was that of *egocentrism* – the tendency of the young child to see things from their own perspective and their inability to take the perspective of others. This concept was followed up and further explored within the field of theory of mind abilities.

Developmental cognitive neuroscience explores brain activity underlying cognitive development in childhood. In contemporary psychology, this area is still very active and productive in terms of the knowledge it is generating about thinking in infancy and early childhood. This area of psychology also supports the notion that close connections exist between action and thinking as when cognitive tasks activate both cognitive control and motor areas of the brain (Diamond, 2000; Miller, 2010). This link between actions and mental representation is supported by the finding that adults' cortical activation is similar when they *perform* a particular action, *think about* performing it or *observe* another person performing that same behaviour (Rizzolatti & Craighero, 2004).

Implications of Piaget's theory of cognitive development for pedagogy in early childhood

1. *Supporting learning both formally and informally in our practice with children.* Piaget's theory of cognitive development in childhood grew

out of his very detailed observations of children's thinking and learning. Understanding how children's thinking changes and develops over time helps us as educators learn how we can best promote and progress children's thinking and cognition.

2. *Helping children make sense and meaning of their experiences.* As we discover some of the key features of children's thinking as they move through infancy and early childhood, we gain insight into the processes through which they make sense and meaning out of novel information and experiences. In this way, early years practitioners can assist in creating rich and resourceful environments in order to guide and support such learning.

3. *Avoiding strategies that might impede or limit the development of children's thinking and learning.* An understanding of children's cognitive development helps us gain greater insight into cognition at other stages of our development. So, for example, through a focus on the features of cognitive development in infancy we can better understand how thinking advances with regard to cognitive development in toddlers and preschoolers.

4. *Processing and interpreting information.* Cognitive development focuses on how we process and interpret information and this is very significant in helping us understand other aspects of children's behaviour. For example, Rachel's actions, and how she cognitively reads those actions as illustrated above, are a source of pleasure for her. On the other hand, Jake reads those same actions in a different way and interprets them as pointless and a source of irritation for him. Through cognitive processing and development children make sense and meaning of the world around them, and these meanings change and expand as children move through early childhood and beyond.

5. *Facilitating and supporting development through play in early childhood.* Three to six years of age has been called the 'golden age of pretend play'. Children engage in fantasies, role plays and acting out adventures through the development of imagination, which is facilitated through language and symbolic representation. All of these important features of childhood experiences are closely linked to the development of cognitive abilities in early childhood. Through a focus on this aspect of children's development, we gain better access to the workings of their minds.

Chapter 3

The building blocks of cognitive development in childhood

Introduction

We have emphasised in chapters 1 and 2 that Piaget saw cognitive development as an active, complex and self-organising system (Miller, 2011). Children do not passively learn from experience. Instead, they actively construct knowledge through interacting with the world and reflecting on these experiences. As Miller states,

> A child knows or understands a ball or a rattle by acting on it – physically or mentally. Infants construct a world of objects to suck, grasp, throw, shake and listen to. It seems impossible today that the 'active child' was a revolutionary notion.
>
> (2011, p. 653)

While Piaget has been criticised for emphasising the somewhat artificial stages of cognitive development, as we will see within this chapter, Piaget also drew attention to certain continuous, ongoing processes that drive cognitive development through childhood and into adulthood. In order to survive in the world around us, we are often called upon to adjust to new situations as, for example, beginning a new course in college, starting a new job and even travelling abroad to a foreign country on holidays. In order to meet the challenges that these new environments place before us, we have to make efforts to adapt to the somewhat unfamiliar elements in these contexts. During infancy and early childhood children are called upon to make sense and meaning of the many new experiences that they encounter. Piaget's theory of cognitive development reflects this pattern of continuous adjustment to new ideas, concepts and meanings. Children adapt to and make sense of new information through their experiences and actions in the world, which ultimately generates a shift to higher functioning within the stages which Piaget described. The child or indeed the adult is all his/her life actively trying to make sense of the world just as any organism must try to adapt to its environment (Meadows, 1993).

Piaget's work made a very significant contribution to helping us gain insight into the processes and mechanisms through which children's thinking develops and increases in competence and complexity. Through a focus on these building blocks of cognitive development we can gain some insight into the mechanisms through which children's processing and interpretation of events in the world around them leads to a more precise understanding of the properties of the world they inhabit. May (2011) provides a lovely example of how young children's minds understand and process information in different ways at different stages of their development. Sometimes, children may come out with what she terms 'misconstructs', while they are in the process of trying to make sense of their worlds. One such example is the reply a 4-year-old girl gave to her mother when asked what she and grandpa had been doing during a morning spent ploughing a field on grandpa's farm with a flock of white birds following the tractor. As May puts it:

> The reply came after a thoughtful pause: 'we were digging up seagulls'.
>
> (2011, p. 22)

Why does the child interpret the event she has witnessed in this way? What aspects of her cognitive processing led her to draw these conclusions about what is happening? One possible explanation is the very young child's inability to *decentre*. What does this mean? According to Piaget the young child can only focus on one aspect of an event at a particular moment in time. In the case of the child described above, it is likely that she was focusing on the machine digging the ground and the birds flying in the air . . . but focusing on these events separately rather than simultaneously. So, for her the digging activity was producing the birds flying in the air because she was not yet able to focus on several aspects of the event at the same time. A second possible reason was that her schemas for birds and other elements of the world around her were not yet fully developed. So, 'digging birds up from the ground' was not yet an impossible event for her.

In order to try to clearly understand the key mechanisms that underlie all of the stages of cognitive development within Piaget's theory, in this chapter we will spend some time unpacking and reflecting on the meanings and principles locked inside the rather complex terms that Piaget used to denote key processes in cognitive development in childhood. We will try to work towards getting a clear and concise outline of these processes, making them accessible through examples and illustrations drawn from working with children in the early years. Key areas to be covered within this chapter include building and expanding schemas, organisation through processes of adaptation, and equilibration. We will also consider how these mechanisms or building blocks pave the way for an understanding of cognitive development in stages as outlined by Piaget. The chapter concludes with an illustration of how Piaget's concept of schemas has further been explored and developed within early childhood education settings.

Principles and mechanisms underpinning Piaget's theory of cognitive development

One of the most well-known and controversial claims that Piaget made was that cognitive development progresses through a series of stages. Each of these stages follows an invariant or unchanging sequence and each stage is characterised by a particular type or way of thinking, reflecting an underlying mental logical structure (Miller, 2011). What Piaget suggests through his theory is that children's thinking is characterised by a particular way of seeing things, depending on the particular cognitive stage they are in. Piaget's structures or set of mental operations can be applied to objects, beliefs or anything in the child's world. It is important to point out that when we speak of a mental structure, we are not talking about a physical part of the brain but rather an organised group of interrelated thoughts and strategies that the child draws on when trying to understand a situation (Parke & Gauvain, 2008). We will look at the detail of Piaget's stages of cognitive development later in this chapter. We will also think about some of the main criticisms that have been directed at his concept of development in cognitive stages. Before we do this, however, it is helpful to consider some more of the terms Piaget used to build his theory.

Building and expanding schemas

As we have outlined above, according to Piaget children organise their knowledge of the world into increasingly more complex cognitive structures (Flavell, 1996). During infancy a cognitive structure is called a *schema* – a framework that organises information related to the child's experience at a particular time (Miller, 2011) – a cluster of ideas/concepts associated with a particular experience. Schemas gradually evolve from those in infancy based on actions to those based on representations in early childhood and to those based on internalised, organised operations in middle childhood.

Let's take an example of a schema in practice.

Charlie (2 years, 4 months) has a simple schema for dogs that includes information such as 'four-legged' and 'moving'. When Charlie sees a horse for the first time, therefore, he points to it and calls it 'big doggie'.

However, with experience, and parallel to Charlie's increasing capacity for classifying and categorising objects, he will learn to identify and name the many different types of animals he encounters. In this way, children's schemas are constantly expanding and adjusting to reflect the dynamic and ever-changing nature of their understanding of the world around them. To return to our example of Charlie building a schema for 'dogs', on seeing a cat for the first time, Charlie wonders why some dogs have whiskers and others do not. Motivated by his experience and enquiring mind, Charlie eventually learns that 'dogs', 'cats' and 'horses' all belong within a broader schema for 'animals'.

So, we can see clearly that Piaget's schemas are not static but rather evolving structures, in other words, structures that expand and change as we encounter new experiences and knowledge. As children's schemas expand, so too does their ability to classify and categorise objects and events in the world around them and we will return to these in more detail within each of Piaget's four stages of cognitive development.

A simple way of explaining what we mean by a schema is to compare it to a folder on a computer – something we use to organise or cluster together documents that have a common theme. So, as an adult you may have a schema for air travel that includes check in, luggage, departures desk, boarding pass, boarding gate, etc. Applying the notion of schemas to development in infancy, Miller (2011) goes on to illustrate this through a focus on the sucking schema, which describes the way infants put various objects into their mouths and suck them. As the schema develops and becomes more differentiated, children classify objects into *suckables* and *non-suckables*, with various sub-categories such as hard suckables, soft suckables and good-tasting suckables. In a similar way, the evolution of schemas for 'picking up' and 'grasping' are illustrated in the following observations of Abbie recorded in her day-care setting.

- Abbie (8 months) crawls towards 'Hoppy', her favourite toy, a rather worn but soft and comforting toy kangaroo. Once nearby, she reaches out and picks him up in a single movement.
- Abbie, sitting on Lucy's (early years practitioner) lap, reaches for her bottle on the table with one hand. Unable to grasp it sufficiently in order to lift it to her mouth, the bottle topples over. Lucy comforts her and hands her the bottle, supporting it as Abbie brings it to her mouth.
- Abbie, sitting in her high-chair, reaches out for her bottle with two hands and slowly lifts it to bring it to her mouth.

These observations of Abbie's behaviours provide us with an illustration of how schemas can help her to direct and tailor her actions in a way that ultimately allows her more control over the objects she comes into contact with. Abbie has developed the schema for 'picking up' and has learned from her experiences that Hoppy can be picked up easily with one hand. However, other objects, such as her bottle when full of milk, require both hands and more effort on her part. Over time, her schema for 'picking up' will become modified into different schemas that accommodate the realities and properties (soft, hard, heavy, light) of different objects, so that she may have a schema for things that cannot be picked up because they are too hot or too heavy (Santrock, 2011). Progressively, these schemas become increasingly organised, as when sucking and grasping schemas are eventually organised into a higher order structure that allows coordinated reaching for an object and bringing it to the mouth to suck (Miller, 2011).

For now, it is sufficient for us to understand schemas as:

- basic building blocks in Piaget's theory;
- clusters of ideas/concepts associated with an experience;
- similar to folders in which we organise material on our computers;
- evolving and expanding over time to include novel information;
- becoming more and more complex in their organisation as experience throws up new information that will be classified and further structured and ordered within hierarchies of knowledge.

On an outing with the crèche, James sees a crow and a pigeon in the sky and his key worker Keith explains that they are birds. James forms a bird schema, which he defines as 'something that flies'. On the following day, James goes to the beach with his family and here he spots a seagull, a good match for his existing bird schema. This is called assimilation when we take new experiences/knowledge and put them in our existing schemas.

Back in the crèche on the following Monday, James is playing outside and sees a plane in the sky. Even though the plane fits his 'something that flies' folder, it appears that this is rather different than the other birds he has seen, and Keith tells him that this is not a bird. James has now formed one expanded schema for 'flying things', which has two sub-categories: birds and planes. This process is called accommodation, where we change our existing knowledge structures to account for new information that does not fit.

Organisation – coordinating and combining

May (2011) likens the child's mind to a jigsaw that the child is constructing based on their experiences, abilities and interests. The child's schemas are a powerful resource and tool to enable the child to fill in more pieces of the jigsaw. Piaget used the term 'organisation' to refer to the inborn capacity to coordinate existing cognitive structures, or schemas, and combine them into more complex systems. For example, the baby of 3 months has learned to combine looking and grasping with the earlier reflex of sucking. She can do all three together when feeding, an ability that the new-born baby did not have (Smith *et al.*, 2003).

Jamie (3 years) has learned to carry things without dropping them, to pour liquid into containers and to reach upwards in order to grasp objects. At lunchtime in his day-care setting, Jamie now combines these three abilities to help serve lunch to the children at his table. He carefully reaches up to take the jug of juice from the shelf, carries the jug to the table and pours juice into the four tumblers for the children at his table. Each separate operation combines into a new action that is more complex than the sum of its parts (Smith *et al.*, 2003).

Adaptation – making sense of the world

Making sense of the world involves an ongoing effort on the part of the child to adapt to characteristics of the environment. Piaget throws a spotlight on the central mechanism through which children's understanding and thinking progresses to more complex levels – *adaptation*. Children adapt their schemas based on experiences with the world. Jamie has adapted his schemas for carrying and pouring in order to be able to assist in serving lunch.

Adaptation is achieved through two further mechanisms

Assimilation – the process through which children incorporate new information into an existing schema.
Accommodation – the process through which children change or adjust their schemas in order to accommodate new information.

Miller (2011) points out that a child's mind is not like a camera but that experience is always filtered through the child's current ways of understanding. Accommodation occurs because the current structures have failed to interpret an object or event satisfactorily. Charlie found it difficult to assimilate 'whiskers' into his schema for dogs. The cognitive adjustment Charlie eventually made in his recognition that dogs and cats are two different types of animals facilitated a more advanced level of understanding of his world. Because we are adults and because we have accommodated much of our environment into complex schemas, we do not typically have to adjust our schemas to fit with our environments, unless we come across original and unfamiliar events and objects. Consequently, it might be a little difficult for us to understand the processes of assimilation and accommodation in practice. However, for the young child, especially the child in its first year, the environment is a process of discovery and adventure, and learning to understand and have some control over this environment is a challenging task for the infant and young toddler. During these early years the processes of assimilation and accommodation are likely to be operating continuously to update mental images and understandings of the world and to reflect more accurately the properties of the surrounding environment.

One example of how we as adults have to accommodate new concepts and experiences is how we have shifted our concept of what a mobile phone is used for since the advent of smartphones. No longer are phones just for contacting friends and texting messages but now we can use them for email, internet surfing, Twitter, Facebook and they can be used to store music, books and films.

So, a central concept within Piaget's theory is that cognitive abilities develop in a way that reflects more generally the adaptation between living things and their environments that we see in the world around (Meadows, 1993). This adaptation in cognitive development proceeds by means of the twin processes of assimilation (relating new information to pre-existing structures of knowledge and understanding) and accommodation (developing the old structures into new ones under pressure from new, externally-given information). In the following sections we will spend more time reflecting on the processes of assimilation and accommodation and apply them to practical examples of working with young children in the early years.

We can see from these examples that children are constantly seeking to achieve a balance between the physical world around them and the perceived world achieved through cognitive processing. As Smith *et al.* put it:

> Assimilation helps the child to consolidate mental structures; accommodation results in growth and change. All adaptation contains components of both processes and striving for balance between assimilation and accommodation results in the child's intrinsic motivation to learn. When new experiences are close to the child's capacity to respond, then conditions are at their best for change and growth to occur.
>
> (2003, p. 393)

Axel (10 months) can manage to get baby food to his mouth with his hand with confidence. But now he tries to eat with a spoon. He scoops up the food successfully, but what goes to his mouth is the spoon handle; the food ends up on his forehead. Later, after weeks of practice, Alex can eat successfully with the spoon.

> On a visit to the local church, Tess (4 years, 6 months) stops to look at the headstones of some old graves that are located on the grounds. She observes that they have groups of numbers (1809–1867). She tries to understand them based on what she already knows about numbers grouped that way. Then she looks perplexed and says, 'But you can't really call them, can you, if they're dead?' Her key worker Joanne explains that these are not phone numbers, but dates and goes on to demonstrate how dates are written.

Equilibration – in pursuit of balance

At times children come face to face with situations that demand skills beyond their current level of development. The result for the child is a state of cognitive disequilibrium or imbalance. The pursuit of a balance between the actual, physical world and the mental representation of the physical world drives the child's learning and development to ever-increasing complexity. As we have emphasised, Piaget tended to use some very complex terms when describing some of the processes in children's cognitive development. One of these terms is *equilibration*. Piaget proposed that children's thinking shifted to more complex levels of thinking through a mechanism that he termed equilibration – the interactions and outcomes of ongoing cycles of assimilation and accommodation.

Imagine what would happen if children could only assimilate and never accommodate – everything new we encountered would just get put in the same few files we already had or vice versa, if we could only accommodate but not assimilate. The result would be confusing to say the least, as everything we encountered would seem new and there would be no recurring regularities in our world.

Therefore, there needs to be a balance between the two processes.

Equilibrium is a balance between assimilation and accommodation.
Disequilibrium is an imbalance between assimilation and accommodation.

When disequilibrium occurs, the learner seeks equilibrium; that is, to further assimilate or accommodate. Let us explore an example:

> Matthew (age 3) is playing at the water table, when the room manager Eric arrives carrying a bag with something that appears to be very heavy in it. Eric explains that he has brought some pebbles and small rocks for Matthew to play with in the water. 'See what happens when you throw them in', says Eric encouragingly. Matthew takes a few

pebbles and throws them in. He has done this before and he knows that they will sink to the bottom. But then, Eric brings out another slightly bigger rock, it's a pumice rock. Pumice is a porous, volcanic rock and it is so light that it floats. 'See what happens when you throw this rock in', says Eric. 'The rock floats!' Matthew has no schema for a floating rock. Toy boats float, but rocks are meant to sink. The new information leads to a state of disequilibrium and Matthew finds himself with three options:

1. He can take the rock into the next room, return and pretend it never existed.
2. He can choose to exclude the differences in appearance between the toy boat and the strange rock and assimilate it into his 'toy boat' schema.
3. His third choice is to make a slight change in his current rock schema by accommodating the new information, and modify his understanding of rocks.

When children's behaviour matches the demands of their environment, they are in a state of equilibrium. The child's natural response to disequilibrium, according to Piaget, is to try to bring things back into equilibrium by an ongoing process of adaptation through assimilation and accommodation.

So, to summarise, equilibration is the process through which children question their knowledge and understanding of the world based on their experiences and in this way, review and update their schemas. When children are adjusting to new experiences and the knowledge that those experiences generate, they may experience what is known as 'cognitive dissonance' or 'cognitive conflict' (disequilibrium) as they struggle to fit new knowledge into what is already known (May, 2011). Over time, and with experience of the world, the child resolves the conflict and reaches a balance, or equilibrium of thought. Piaget believed that there is considerable movement between states of cognitive equilibrium and disequilibrium as assimilation and accommodation work in concert to produce cognitive change (Santrock, 2011).

Building blocks to cognitive development in stages

Schemas, adaptation through assimilation and accommodation and equilibration are key building blocks in Piaget's stage theory of cognitive development in childhood. For Piaget, these processes were at work consistently and at all times – a process that is both iterative and cyclical in its pattern. One of the very distinctive characteristics of Piaget's model of cognitive development is the notion that thinking and understanding does not progress in an altogether gradual and smooth fashion, but rather abilities and competences *expand* at some stages and *plateau* or level out at other stages of development. Intellectual growth was viewed in terms of progressive changes in children's cognitive structures and these changes manifest themselves in stages of development, with each stage being different from the one that precedes it. All children according to Piaget develop through the same sequence of stages before achieving mature, rational thought (Wood, 1998). The structure of children's thinking at each stage is distinctive, the same for all children at that stage and different from that of children and adults of other stages. As Wood puts it:

> Development for Piaget is not simply the continuous accumulation of things learned step by step. Rather it involves a number of intellectual 'revolutions' at specific junctures in the life-cycle, each one of which involves important changes in the structure of intelligence. Each stage yields a different way of thinking about and understanding the world from that which it grows out of and replaces.
>
> (1998, p. 52)

One of the principles that Piaget's stage theory generated was the notion of 'readiness to learn' in education – in other words, the child must be 'ready' to move on to the next developmental stage and cannot be forced to move to a higher level of cognitive functioning. While developmental stages can be useful in guiding how we plan children's learning, they have also been criticised as limiting and constraining children's abilities (Young-Ihm, 2002). More broadly, we need to integrate pedagogical knowledge with knowledge about children's development and with information about the nature of knowledge itself (Young-Ihm, 2002). Piaget's main contribution is, perhaps, that his focus on cognitive development in particular and the detailed observations that accompanied and supported his theory allowed early childhood education practitioners to tailor the learning environment and develop strategies that facilitated effective learning. Similarly, Vygotsky drew attention to the zone of proximal development which provides a focus on supporting the child to move beyond the abilities they have in order to solve problems by themselves.

Stage theories had influenced approaches to early childhood education in advance of Piaget's theory. Central to educational planning in a Montessori approach is consideration of developmental stages and sensitive periods so that early childhood education practitioners can generate learning opportunities tailored to meet the needs of children during these stages. The Steiner-Waldorf model of early childhood education also drew attention to stages or phases of development with the years before adulthood being schematically broken up into three 7-year cycles.

Piaget's stages of cognitive development

Four stages of cognitive development were identified by Piaget and within these stages a number of substages were also identified. These four key stages are briefly outlined in Table 3.1.

Challenges to Piaget's stage theory of cognitive development

Piaget's theory of cognitive development has been criticised on many levels and we will look at these comprehensively throughout the book and draw conclusions for practice with young children. Most immediately, we will reflect a little on why a stage theory of cognitive development has been

Table 3.1 Piaget's stages of cognitive development

Stage	Age	Key features
Sensorimotor	Birth to 2 years	The very young child in infancy learns through their actions in the world and the sensory feedback that is generated through these actions.
Preoperational	2–7 years	Children move from the physical, concrete world to a more symbolic understanding of the world around them. As children move through this stage, these symbols become increasingly organised and logical so that children can think more effectively about causes.
Concrete operational	7–11 years	Logical thinking becomes more complex and refined, allowing more flexibility in thinking processes. The ability to think in the abstract also increases, although actions are still the main source of knowledge. However, these actions can now be carried out in mental operations. Children no longer understand properties based on appearance only but understand that quantities stay the same even though they change their appearance.
Formal operational	11–15 years	Adolescents have the ability to think more effectively using abstract ideas and through hypothetical thinking.

questioned and challenged. As those of us working with young children know, children do not actually change so dramatically from one day to another in terms of their cognitive abilities. That is not to say that there are not dramatic changes in development – of course, we know there are. There are changes that we might term as being qualitative rather than quantitative – such as the change when a child utters their first word. However, below we summarise some of the main limitations that have been generated in response to Piaget's stage theory and we will return to these criticisms in more detail in later chapters.

- It has been argued that Piaget's stages are overly rigid and inflexible and do not reflect the enormous variance in child competence and ability across all ages.
- It has also been argued that Piaget's stage theory of cognitive development underestimated certain cognitive competencies in children. Many later theorists argued that some of the tasks that Piaget used to assess these abilities were not child-friendly and that children perform better when the task is better tailored to their interests and contexts.
- Piaget himself used the term 'invariant' when talking about his stages. Yet research has also shown that children do not necessarily acquire concepts and broad conceptual structures that apply to all content areas. Significantly, Piaget himself later acknowledged that children do not acquire concepts across all content areas when he used the term 'horizontal décalage' – a French term that roughly translated means a 'horizontal lag' – and implies that a general concept may emerge earlier on some tasks than on others.
- The context of learning may influence the extent to which a child develops a certain concept. A good illustration of this is that infants are more likely to demonstrate the concept of object permanence when the object is the mother rather than a physical object (Bell, 1970; Miller, 2011). Post-Piagetian research has also identified that children are more likely to succeed in tasks that reflect the child's interests and with which the child is familiar.

So far in this chapter we have grappled with a number of complex terms of relevance to Piaget's theory. We will be returning to these building blocks again and again when we explore the stages of cognitive development as devised by Piaget. We will conclude with some general reflections on the implications of these ideas for working with children in the early years.

Implications for practice

Several important arguments about children's ability to learn flow from Piaget's theory. Most importantly, for the moment, is the notion that what children take away from a particular experience varies according to the stage of development in which this learning is embedded. As Wood puts it:

> Whilst a young child might learn or be taught how to solve a given problem, to provide what sounds like an appropriate answer to a difficult question, or to execute a particular routine (counting or adding numbers) the impact of such experiences on the child will be different in kind from that experienced by one at a later stage of development. The status and significance of what children learn is a direct function of their stage of development.
>
> (1998, p. 52)

In this section we will focus on one of Piaget's concepts outlined above, the concept of schemas, and explore how this concept has been adapted and extended in practice with children in the early years.

Schemas in practice: extending thought in young children

Schema theory has been effectively used in practice within early childhood settings to explore children's deep cognitive and emotional interests and plan for their learning. Athey (1990), whose work has been drawn on substantially for practice in the Pen Green Centre, emphasised the patterns that emerge in children's play and developed the notion that we can extend children's thought through attention to and exploration of their schemas in their play and behaviour. According to Athey (1990), certain patterns of repeatable behaviour can be identified in young children's play. By exploring and practising their schemas in different situations, children become more knowledgeable about the world around them. Some of the most common schemas highlighted within work in the Pen Green Centre include:

Transporting – carrying objects or being carried from one place to another.
Rotation – turning, twisting or rolling themselves or objects.
Containing – putting themselves or objects or materials into different containers.
Envelopment – covering themselves, objects or a space.

A more comprehensive list of schemas is provided by Athey (1990). Paffard (2010) also talks of the benefits for early years practitioners of attending to the different concepts that children are exploring through schemas. For example, evidence of an enclosure schema may be noted as the child fills boxes with small objects such as beads, and then spends as much time as possible in a 'cave' or a tent and perhaps makes patterns with edges and borders. Athey (1990) and other authors drew attention to the fact that attending to schemas in children's play was a useful way to help us understand a child's motivation for doing something.

- Based on schemas identified in children's behaviour, we can extend their learning by matching curriculum content based on their individual interests. Close attention to the schemas in children's play and activities enables educators to work with children and interact with them in a helpful way, respectful of their individual interests.
- Schema theory has also been adapted for work with children with special needs. When we consider that young children, especially in the first two years of their lives, learn and develop primarily in a sensorimotor world and are dependent on the feedback provided by their actions on that physical world, we can understand that, for example, the visually or hearing-impaired child may not have access to the wealth of knowledge that the environment feeds back to them. Such children may be typically unaware of the range of play opportunities that exist and risk developing a narrow repertoire of movements and routines that give them control within a narrow sphere. Introducing these children to a wider repertoire of schemas in a safe environment could increase their potential to build competence in important domains of their experience.
- Most recently, Cath Arnold at the Pen Green Centre has identified some interesting connections between young children's spontaneous repeated actions and their representations of their emotional worlds. Arnold's (2010) work is a thought-provoking and insightful account of how the cognitive development of the child is inextricably linked to their social and emotional development in early childhood. Based on research carried out alongside children, parents, workers and co-researchers at the Pen Green Centre, and using case studies of a small number of individual children, the author highlights potential links between cognition and affect.

We will return to a consideration of schemas in practice in later chapters of the book.

Chapter 4

The sensorimotor world

Introduction

Piaget's first stage of cognitive development focuses on detailing the pathway from infant awareness, which is almost exclusively reflexive, spontaneous and dependent on sensory motor activities, to a thinking, intentional toddler capable of making things happen in the world around them. According to Piaget, these first two years in infancy can be further divided into six substages of cognitive development. Across these substages, the infant experiences and connects with the world largely through their senses and movement, although progressively developing the ability for symbolic representation as they move through their second year. Much of the infant's learning is generated through intense looking, listening, touching, tasting and smelling, through which they explore and investigate the properties of the concrete world. As they progress through their second year, the infant begins to be able to relate to the world using basic symbols that allow them to represent one object with another. This pattern of symbolic development is supported through the emergence of language.

The earliest conversations between Jennifer and her mum Vivienne involve the sense of touch. When Vivienne holds Jennifer in her arms, baby nestles against her skin, seeking the perfect fit in the curve of her arms. The skin is the most highly developed sensory organ at birth, and most babies love to be stroked. When Vivienne is applying pressure slowly and gently to baby's skin just before naptime or bedtime, she helps the rather wide-awake baby to settle down.

As Jennifer's grasp becomes more firm, she finds her mother's hair and face an interesting focus of exploration by touch. To Vivienne, this is a sign that her baby is ready for objects with rough, smooth, crinkly, soft and squishy textures – so these are introduced with careful supervision.

Jennifer, like most babies, is born with a sweet tooth, preferring the sweet taste of breast milk or formula to other foods. The other three basic tastes – bitter, sour and salty – develop later. At this stage, Jennifer will have a dislike of bitter tastes, which may protect her from ingesting harmful foods.

Babies can (and will) taste almost anything you give them, and their little hands can't wait to finger whatever comes their way. In fact, a baby's sense of taste and texture work together to help baby make discoveries about the objects in the world.

Born to explore

During the first two years of life, babies actively construct an understanding of the world around them through their actions, movements and the resulting feedback to their senses that these movements bring about. As we have been emphasising throughout previous chapters, development is an active process and babies play an active role in seeking out experiences through which their understanding grows in complexity. Understanding at this stage of development is a gradual process, unfolding over time as described by Gopnik *et al.*

> When we learn about the world, when we do science, for example, we don't just hit the right answer once and for all. Rather, there is a very gradual unfolding sequence of corrected errors, expanded ideas and revised misconceptions as we approach more and more nearly to the truth. That was what the Piagets saw as they watched their babies make their way through infancy.
>
> (2001, p. 16)

In the following short observations taken in day-care settings, we consider three children, each of whom are at different stages of Piaget's sensorimotor world.

Katie is 8 months old. She is in the third substage of Piaget's sensorimotor world. She has just started day-care and is fascinated by all the novel experiences she is encountering. She lies on her cushion and stares at the variety of coloured objects hanging above her head. She reaches out to touch the colourful star, which gently swings when she touches it and makes a tinkling sound. Curious about the sound and movement of the star, she reaches out again and enjoys the soft tinkle it makes as it swings above her.

Exploration is central to learning for the young child, as we can see from these observations. Katie, at only 8 months of age, is motivated from the beginning to discover more about the world in which she finds herself. So, as we already noted, curiosity drives her actions and experiences, motivating her to stare at, listen to, touch and feel things at every opportunity. Through these active explorations, Katie progresses in an orderly way to develop schemas that over time are more effective in representing the external world. She is capable of coordinating schemas – in other words, she has developed a schema for reaching out to touch an object and a schema for pushing an object that she now combines to reach and swing the star above her head.

> Josh is 12 months old. He is in Piaget's fifth substage of sensorimotor– tertiary circular reactions. Like Katie, Josh is curious about all the objects and events in his day-care setting. He has developed schemas that allow him to combine a number of actions. At the moment, he wants to reach out to take his pet blanket. He makes sounds and waves his arms in the direction of his blanket. He crawls towards the blanket and reaching out he grasps and pulls the blanket. The blanket moves slowly but catches against the leg of a chair. Josh pulls more forcefully and manages to capture the blanket.

Josh has all the abilities that Katie demonstrated and more besides. His behaviour is more intentional and purposeful than Katie's. He is very caught up in exploring the world through trial and error. When he wants something, he goes after it and now his schemas have expanded to allow him to combine a number of actions in order to intentionally achieve his goal. If he does not achieve his goal the first time, he will try again and again until he has worked out how to overcome the obstacles in his way.

> Mark is 22 months old and in Piaget's final substage of the sensori- motor world – beginnings of representational thought. Mark is still fascinated by the sensorimotor experiences in his day-care setting. Using paints to splash colour on sheets of paper, exploring objects by climbing into and under them, using words to symbolise these many objects that he is examining. Mark now plays with a colourful crayon box and makes engine sounds as he pushes the box along the ground – he is moving beyond the physical sensory world to the world of symbolic representation and fantasy play.

If we think about the aspects of development documented above in the activities of Katie, Josh and Mark, we become more aware of the unfolding nature of their development and awareness. Through their activities we see an ongoing process of learning through trial and error, correcting those errors and revising the misconceptions that shaped the errors. With each action, schemas are expanded and updated to provide a more accurate picture of the environment.

It is also worth noting the orderliness and agency in the children's development. There is a systematic sequence through which development proceeds. Piaget paid great attention to the orderliness of this process, as we will see in the detail of the pattern of development across his six substages of infant cognitive development. Sensorimotor learning is not random, but is structured, sequenced and supported by the highly individual and active exploration of the infant at the centre of their development.

Before we look at how cognitive abilities unfold through Piaget's sensori-motor stages, we will spend a little time reflecting on the genius of babyhood, as Piaget was one of the first psychologists to investigate the cognitive development of the pre-verbal child.

The genius of babyhood

There is something about infants' ability to make sense of the ever-shifting stimuli around them that conjures up the term 'genius'. As adults we process sensory information without thinking because so much of the sensory information we receive is familiar to us and we have come across it before. But think of the very new baby who sees and hears things, perhaps for the first time, without the refined visual and auditory abilities that we have and who must, therefore, continuously strive to find meanings in the strange and unfamiliar shapes, patterns and sounds that float in and out of their sensory radars.

What makes Piaget stand out from other psychologists before him is the precision of his observations and analyses of young babies' trials, errors and achievements as they gradually unfold across their first two years of life. Smidt (2011) summarises some of the fascinating work that has been carried out with infants over the years since Piaget and Vygotsky set the pace for exploring cognitive development in infancy, and Bruner followed by advancing on their theories. Landmarks such as the Berry Brazelton Neonatal Assessment Scale, Colwyn Trevarthen's work on infant communication, early interactions and emotions, and Hanus Papousek's pioneering work in infant research have contributed significantly to our insight that infants are 'more competent, more active and more organised in their thinking and their behaviour than had been thought before' (Smidt, 2011, p. 29).

Patricia Kuhl, a developmental neuropsychologist from the Institute for Learning and Brain Sciences in the University of Washington, emphasises that currently some of the most revolutionary ideas in brain science are coming from cribs and nurseries. Some fascinating research by Kuhl and her colleagues has shown that up until the age of 6 months, babies can tell the difference between sounds in any language. So, while a Japanese infant can easily distinguish between the sounds /l/ and /r/, a Japanese adolescent or middle-aged parent, can only do this with some difficulty. The genius of babyhood indeed! Significantly, this ability declines rapidly and dramatically after the age of 6 months. Fortunately, there is an upside to this – babies now become much more proficient at tuning into and processing sounds of their own native language. The orderliness of cognitive development, so emphasised by Piaget's theory, is again to be noted in this finding. Something happens around this 6-month milestone that allows infants to become more competent at processing their own language sounds – and simultaneously, they tune out of language sounds that they are not hearing on a regular basis. Brilliant babies indeed!

The path from the world to our brains

As Gopnik *et al.* point out, adults tend to take the meanings and interpretations of the external world for granted – generally not conscious of how 'complicated and torturous the path is from the world to our brains' (2001, p. 62). Making sense of raw sensory information is like decoding a puzzle as the authors express it:

> Our brain takes sensory information, the patterns of stimulation at our retinas and eardrums, and systematically transforms that information. It rearranges and changes it in a way somewhat similar to the way your word processor can rearrange and change the sequence of the symbols you type (though, of course, the brain produces much more complicated rearrangements than the word processor). The outcome of this process is the coherent, complex network of beliefs that are so shockingly challenged by magicians.

The pathway from the world to our brains in infancy is constructed by means of access to sensory and motor information, which the brain decodes and transforms. Sensory information is carefully and precisely filtered and processed by the brain, which selects what information a child needs to know (May, 2011).

Cognitive development through the senses

Piaget emphasised sensorimotor learning in infancy because the infant is exclusively reliant on sensorimotor information for staying connected to the world. Babies are born with sensory and perceptual systems that are programmed to be sensitive to social stimuli such as human voices, faces and smells. Below we highlight some features of sensory learning in infancy that will help us better understand Piaget's substages of sensorimotor development in the first two years of life.

- Babies' vision at birth is approximately 8–12 inches in range: just sufficient to allow the infant to be able to see the mother's face when feeding.
- Infants as young as 12 hours old have been observed to spend more time looking at their mother's face when compared with a stranger's face. This preference is usually investigated after the baby has been separated from his or her mother for a few minutes and can be apparent after only an hour's attention to her face, though it gets stronger with greater experience.
- During the first month after birth, infants' scanning patterns change dramatically until at the age of 2–3 months their scanning is similar to that of older children and adults (Santrock, 2011).
- Young babies like patterns such as stripes and more complex patterns rather than simple or plain surfaces. The reason for this is that babies like the contrast between the brightness and texture of two surfaces, as this usually indicates where objects begin and end (Gopnik *et al.*, 2001).

Why are these early sensory abilities so central to the baby's interaction with the world? The simple answer is that the baby's responsiveness to sensory information in the environment – for example, gazing into a mother's eyes – provides evidence for caregivers that the child is aware of them and interested in their attention. Being able to elicit a positive response from adult caregivers is, of course, a very important requirement that enhances the baby's safety and wellbeing.

Cognitive development through movement

Even before infants have begun to move themselves, we know that there is a lot of movement in the world around them and, naturally, this movement impacts on how they see and experience the world. Movement is a valuable source of knowledge for young babies who have not yet developed the ability to raise themselves, reach for objects and crawl or toddle towards them. In time they will develop abilities to move independently, to crawl towards an attractive toy, to stand up and reach for an object that catches their attention. Increased motor abilities make it possible for the infant to engage in greater object exploration and investigation, paving the way for more precise under-standing of the properties of objects. Movement also allows the young child to get further knowledge about shape and size constancy. As we move around in the environment, our perspective on an object changes. For example, the farther away we are from an object, the smaller that object appears to us. A table will look different to us depending on whether we are sitting at the table, or under the table! They young child crawling and exploring learns shape and size constancy through these actions. You may be wondering how this information is related to Piaget's theory of cognitive development in the first two years of life, but hopefully this will become clearer as we move on to focus on the detail of Piaget's sensorimotor stage.

Six stages of sensorimotor experience

Piaget was very interested in exploring how the young infant progresses from a world in which events seem to happen by accident to a world where infants are instrumental in making things happen as they increase their understanding of cause and effect in the environment. Piaget mapped out this development on to six substages of the sensorimotor stage. Two patterns are worth noting as we move through these substages:

- Infants adapt their schemas to an increasingly expanding range of situations and experiences.
- Activity in the external, physical world is increasingly represented mentally through symbols in the second year of the sensorimotor world.

> Clara is 2 weeks old. When her mother touches her cheek softly, Clara turns her head in the direction of the sensation. When her mother places her finger in Clara's palm, Clara closes her fingers tightly around the finger. Changes in the sound of the washing machine whirring nearby startle her and her head turns in reaction to these sudden and unexpected noises.

Stage 1: Reflexes (birth to 1 month): flexing muscles

This first stage of cognitive development covers the first 4 weeks of the infant's life. According to Piaget, the infant's capabilities in the first month of life are largely understood in terms of reflex action. The infant may grasp a finger placed in its palm, and respond to a light touch on the cheek by 'rooting' around or blink in response to a puff of air (DeHart *et al.*, 2004). All of these simple, reactive behaviours provide building blocks for the development of increasingly flexible sensorimotor schemes.

- Clara reacts to physical stimuli such as turning in response to a sensation on her cheek or to a change in sound, grasping a finger placed in her palm.

Stage 2: Primary circular reactions (1 to 4 months): look at me!

> Clara is lying in her cot. She gazes at her mother's face when she interacts with her. She moves her arms around repeatedly and eventually brings her hand to her mouth. Having carried out this action several times, Clara eventually puts her thumb in her mouth and begins to suck her thumb.

This second sensorimotor stage is characterised by the infant's curiosity about and exploration of movements, focusing on its own body. At first, behaviours occur by accident, but over time the infant intentionally repeats actions that produce a pleasing outcome. The term 'primary' refers to the fact that the infant is centring its actions and attentions on itself and not on the external world. The word 'circular' refers to actions that are repeated intentionally. The reflexive actions that we saw in the first sensorimotor stage set the stage for these primary circular reactions.

- Clara can actively explore her world through movement of her arms, staring at her feet, sucking her thumb.
- Clara has not yet begun to explore the external world but focuses all her actions on herself at the moment.

Stage 3: Secondary circular reactions (4 to 8 months): making things happen

> Clara is 6 months old now. She is curious about everything she sees and hears around her. She watches intently as her mum loads clothes into the washing machine on the other side of the room. Clara now stares at small objects that attract her attention. She can stretch out both hands to grasp a small toy of interest. She grasps her rattle and bangs it on the counter. When her brother approaches her with a new toy, Clara immediately drops the first toy and grasps this new object. If an object drops from her hand but remains in sight, she will stare at the object where it has fallen. However, if an object falls out of her sight, she may momentarily search with hands or eyes, but soon loses interest.

Adventurous, exploratory behaviour accelerates during this Piagetian stage and the infant's connections to the outside world become more accessible. The term 'secondary' here refers to the fact that Clara's actions are now directed at objects external to her while 'circular' once again refers to the fact that the action is repeated. 'Reactions' refers to Clara's shaking the rattle as a reaction to hearing the sound. In secondary circular reactions, infants actively experience the effects of their behaviours on external objects. Babies kick out their legs to touch a mobile, which in turn produces a tinkling sound. Babies wave their arms to touch a rattle in order to repeat the pleasant sound it gives off when shaken or touched. The most important difference between this stage and primary circular reactions is that actions are now centred on objects and people in the *external* world. This is a dramatic achievement for the infant. During these months the joy of exploration and of being able to *make things happen* drives the infant to play and experiment with everything within reach.

- Clara can now make an effect on the external world.
- Clara is learning pairings between her own behaviour and sensory consequences.
- Some early forms of imitation can be identified in this stage as, for example, when Clara makes a gurgling sound, her brother imitates her, and Clara gurgles back in response. Imitation is limited to behaviours that Clara can already perform; the ability to copy new behaviours is not yet present.
- Although Clara can make certain things happen in the world around her, Piaget did not consider these behaviours intentional.
- Clara has now moved from single schemas, for example the schema for grasping, to combinations of schema, such as grasping and shaking her rattle.

Stage 4: Coordination of schemes (8 to 12 months):
planning adventures

Clara is 10 months old now and has been in day-care for the past 2 months. She is attracted to the many colourful objects and toys in her setting. Her favourite musical book lies across the room half obscured by a soft cushion. Linda, her key worker, watches Clara who spends a little time looking around and eventually crawls towards her musical book. 'Good girl Clara! You're going to get your book!' Clara smiles and before reaching for her book she pushes the cushion aside. She then grasps her musical book, immediately pressing the sound buttons to hear the resulting music.

Adventure and exploration now become more intentional or purposeful as the infant can *combine* some of the previous behaviours in order to expand its ability to make an effect on the world. In this stage, Clara is beginning to put actions together into goal-directed chains of behaviour, which Piaget called *coordination of schemes*. Goal directed is a rather complex term, which simply means that the baby's actions now have a distinct purpose and objective to them. During this stage, the key developmental milestone for the infant in Piaget's view was intentionality – deliberate planning for the attainment of a goal. Clara now has the ability to anticipate the future consequences of her actions and a new dimension to her actions is that of *purposefulness*. A very typical example of a milestone achievement during this fourth substage is the ability of infants to feed themselves, which involves coordinating a series of actions in order to produce a desired outcome. Piaget believed that between 8 and 12 months the young child achieves object permanence – the knowledge that an object exists although it is no longer in sight.

- Clara is motivated to actively explore through sensory actions and movement.
- Clara can now carry out an action that she has anticipated or intended to carry out.
- Clara can coordinate her actions with greater efficiency so that she can combine a number of actions in order to achieve a goal.
- Clara is learning to solve problems through her actions; for example, pushing something aside in order to access an object that was obstructed.

Stage 5: Tertiary circular reactions (12 to 18 months): trial and error experiments

Clara is 15 months old. She is playing in the 'curiosity corner' of her day-care setting. Lots of interesting objects are provided – soft velvet, colourful materials, crisp, crackly papers, tubs of sand and tubs of pasta shells, large and small soft animal toys, books with buttons to press in order to make sounds both loud and soft. Mirrors on the wall reflect the colours and shapes of the objects. Clara, at present, is fascinated by the way in which the pasta shells clatter out into a heap when she pours them on to the surface. She raises herself to find out what happens when she pours them out from a height. Now they scatter about before they fall to the ground. By contrast, when she pours the tub of sand out on to the surface, it spreads silently across the surface.

As with primary and secondary circular reactions, a tertiary reaction begins when some action accidentally leads to an interesting sensory consequence. Infants at this stage experiment and rather than just repeating the action, they

now vary the action in some way in order to explore the possible consequences. Clara varies the way in which she empties the pasta shells – at first
while sitting down and then from a height as she stands up. Infant scientists
are relentless in their quest for new information about the objects they are
encountering. Clara is engaging in early problem solving, which is helping
her to accommodate to her environment and also helping her to assimilate
her ever-changing schemas. These trial-and-error variations allow her to
discover new cause-and-effect relationships. We can see that Clara is gaining
more and more control over her knowledge and learning. As a result of her
experimenting, her understanding of the environment is expanding, informed
by the feedback that each of her trial-and-error activities generates.

- Clara no longer repeats actions but can vary her actions in order to find
  out more about an object.
- Clara can maintain interest in objects for longer, which allows her to try
  out different actions.
- Clara is becoming more expert about the properties of objects. For
  example, hard objects make a loud sound when dropped on to a hard
  surface. Soft objects fall on to the ground silently.
- Clara is learning new ways of solving problems and rather than repeating
  actions as she did in the previous substage, she now moves beyond to
  discover new actions that work for her.

*Stage 6: Beginnings of representational thought (18 to
24 months): storing up experience*

Clara is almost 2 years old. Judy has set up the room for some sensory
activities for the children, many of whom are some months younger
than Clara. Clara is enjoying working on the playdough, squeezing it,
pulling it, throwing it down on the table, stretching it and generally
engrossed in making shapes with it. Her playmates finger the dough
and stare at it for long periods; another child is absorbed in putting it
in dots about the floor, while others explore how it smells and feels on
their skin and in their hair. Clara is now forming her playdough into the
shape of a ball. Out of the blue, she stretches her arm out to show Judy
her playdough ball and smilingly exclaims: 'BUN!'

Clara's ability to represent a bun with her playdough ball illustrates that
she can now enjoy and communicate through symbols, an ability that is
supported through the emergence of language abilities. In contrast to the
younger children, who are engrossed in the physical sensations of working
with the playdough, Clara mentally represents this physical world internally

and, in turn, draws on this mental representation to make a 'playdough bun'. Piaget described his final sensorimotor stage as the start of the transition from sensorimotor to symbolic or representational thought – the ability to make one thing stand for another, to represent one object using another object. Children frequently inhabit the pretend world from this point onwards – boxes become cars, building blocks become smartphones held to the ear and monologue conversations ensue; dolls as babies are fed by putting spoons to the mouth and pretend feeding. Symbolic thought allows the child to pretend to be whoever they wish to be in their socio-dramatic play activities. Clara is now capable of what Piaget termed *deferred imitation* – she no longer depends on the presence of an action in order to be able to imitate but has somehow acquired the ability to store the memory of a behaviour and retrieve it through her own behaviour at a later point. The key change is that Clara can now internalise and mentally represent images. Piaget believed that children achieve full understanding of object permanence during this final substage, which allows them to search for a hidden object in the correct locations.[1]

- Clara can now mentally represent and store information.
- Clara can better plan to solve problems because objects and people can be represented symbolically.
- Imitation becomes more apparent as information from previous observations is now stored and retrieved when necessary.

One of the most interesting developments for children from this point onwards is their involvement and exploration through pretend play. May (2011) describes how children will hold long conversations 'in role' about bathing the baby or driving the train – what is so enjoyable and beneficial about these experiences is that they allow children to rehearse roles that are well beyond their capacity in real life, but easily achievable in the world of pretend.

Object permanence – out of sight, out of mind

> Perhaps young infants, brand new in the world, experience their environment as a kind of nonsensical dream in which even the simplest properties of objects surprise them. Wow, they wonder, where does the world go to when I close my eyes?
>
> (PsyBlog, 2008, n)

Piaget was the first psychologist to draw attention to the concept of object permanence in infants. This is a key milestone achieved in the final substage of sensorimotor infancy. Object permanence, as the terms suggests to us, is the understanding that objects continue to exist even when they can no longer be seen. This concept is further explained, developed and illustrated in chapter 5. According to Piaget (1954) object permanence is gradually constructed and different aspects of this understanding emerge between 8 and 18 months, when Piaget believed the infant had developed full understanding of this construct.

However, more recent research, most notably by Renee Baillargeon and her colleagues, indicates that babies as young as 3½ months or even younger may understand object permanence (Baillargeon *et al.*, 2011). Some of the criticisms of Piaget's tasks exploring object permanence were that they demanded motor actions that younger infants were not capable of. So, for example, it was suggested that if the baby had been able to crawl or physically reach out to search for the object, they might show greater ability to retrieve an object and greater understanding of object permanence.

So, later research building on and amending Piaget's experiments suggested that it was the infant's lack of motor activity that prevented them from demonstrating their awareness of object permanence. For now, we just need to know that Piaget believed this understanding and awareness evolved gradually. In the following chapter, we will discuss some of the implications of object permanence for babies and children in early childhood. These include the associated ability of being able to mentally represent objects and people and store this image in memory. Such a development is interesting to reflect on in light of children's attachment to parents, siblings and caregivers, and to infants' growing security in the belief that their parents will return when no longer in sight.

Update on the sensorimotor stage

We know that there has been much criticism and questioning of Piaget's beliefs about children's abilities. Piaget was very careful not to attribute abilities to children unless they could be clearly supported by empirical research with these children. However, as we will see in later chapters, many of the tasks that Piaget developed to assess children's cognitive abilities were judged to be overly complex and often not clearly relevant to the child's experience. For example, as noted above, tasks exploring the development of an understanding of object permanence did not take into account the young child's ability to move and reach out for an object. Much research has been carried out to further explore some of the findings that Piaget came up with in his cognitive developmental tasks. In the following sections we highlight three areas where Piaget's theory on sensorimotor learning has been updated:

Object permanence

As we have already noted, much work has focused on replicating experiments to do with establishing at what age infants become aware of the concept of object permanence. We will reserve discussion of recent and current research in this area – some of which has contested Piaget's view – and claim that infants acquire object permanence understanding and awareness in the first months of their lives.

Intentional thinking and behaviour

We have seen that it was only during the very last substages of the sensori-motor stage that Piaget believed that babies could plan their actions in a way that suggested that they had the ability to form a mental representation of the event. In the 1980s some interesting experiments by Willatts suggested that babies can mentally represent information and plan activities based on this mental representation as early as 9 months of age. Such work involved placing a toy that was attractive to the baby beyond reach of the baby. Psychologists are cruel, we have noted before! However, fortunately for the babies, the attractive toy was placed on a cloth (so the baby could pull the cloth to move the toy closer to them). Unfortunately for the babies, the cruel psychologists then placed a light barrier between the child and the cloth. What was surprising in the results of this experiment was that these very young 9-month-old babies were able to coordinate a sequence of actions in order to achieve their goal. The babies first moved the barrier and then pulled the cloth with the attractive toy within their reach. The genius of babyhood once more confirmed! Willatts (1989) demonstrated further that, not only did these 9-month-old infants demonstrate the ability to coordinate their actions to achieve this goal, they were able to do this the first time they encountered this problem. This suggested that they had a mental representation of the external world and could draw on this mental representation, rather than trial-and-error experiments with objects, to guide their systematic actions to achieve their goal.

Deferred imitation

Piaget believed that babies can imitate early in their first few months certain behaviours present and accessible to them – for example, if a caregiver smiles at them or makes a strange face, the baby may attempt to imitate. However, in Piaget's theory, babies can only imitate actions – i.e. a caregiver sticking out their tongue – as long as that behaviour is present and visible to them. For Piaget, imitation based on a stored mental representation of a particular behaviour emerged much later in infancy. In some more recent work with infants carried out by Meltzoff and Moore (1994), 6-week-old infants were exposed to adults making faces at them. In this case some infants were exposed to an adult sticking out her tongue at them, while other infants saw the adult's facial expression, which was neutral. The following day all the children saw the same adult again, but on this occasion the adult maintained a passive face. Compared with children who had not seen any gesture, the infants who had seen the adult sticking out their tongue were more likely to imitate these behaviours the second time they saw her. Meltzoff and Moore (1994) argued that if the babies were able to imitate behaviour based on what they had seen on a previous day, they must, therefore, be able to store mental representations at a much earlier age than Piaget had suggested.

Implications for practice

We can see from Piaget's substages that babies are extremely competent from birth and that competence steadily increases throughout infancy. Despite the fact that some of Piaget's estimated ages for achievement for certain tasks have been revised, the detail he provides about the development of such important milestones as object permanence, intentional behaviour, mental representation and symbolic thought helps to guide early years practitioners in promoting and supporting these emerging abilities in the young infant. In the following sections we will consider some of the implications of Piaget's theory and detail of the substages of the sensorimotor world. In particular, we will provide a focus on how early years practitioners can design and develop safe and appropriate environments for the very young infant and child.

1. The importance of sensory and motor pathways to learning in these first two years is emphasised in Piaget's first stage. Creating opportunities for the very young baby to have access to visual and auditory stimuli will undoubtedly provide pleasure and motivation to further explore. The importance of space for the young infant to crawl and move around in supervised safety is also highlighted in this sensorimotor period. Bradford (2012) provides some insightful ideas for developing appropriate environments for infants and toddlers in day-care settings. The importance of including a number of distinct and separate areas for the young child to explore is emphasised. The central importance of discovery learning through trial and error in interactions with the environment is also foregrounded in Piaget's sensorimotor stage of development. Young infants, especially from 8 months onwards, increase their knowledge and understanding by trying out actions with objects – letting things fall, banging hard and soft objects, making sounds and shapes. May (2011) points out that children can be encouraged to examine interesting objects such as clocks that tick, flowers that open or feathers that drift to the ground. Some ideas that are well aligned to Piaget's sensorimotor substages are outlined by Bradford (2012).

   • An *active physical play* area that can meet the child's need for mobility in all directions, from allowing the child to lie, kick and stretch on a play mat to learning to take first steps to being able to sit, stand or move around, pushing and moving objects from one place to another.

- A *manipulative play area* that offers the child opportunities to explore and discover how things work, how to make an effect on things and how to solve simple problems.
- A *curiosity/sensory corner* that supports and promotes the child's need to discover, explore, touch and experience a wide range of materials.

2. When working with very young babies, the importance of communication and interaction cannot be over-emphasised. As Piaget highlighted, the young infant is naturally motivated to connect with others in the world and to explore the properties of things and objects from the earliest months, especially once into the secondary circular reactions stage. Communication, however, begins at birth and the early years practitioner will learn invaluable information about the individual needs of the young child through detailed listening to and observation of the sounds, movements and actions of individual babies. Opportunities for talking and listening to the baby abound through routines of feeding, changing and soothing when settling babies down for sleep. Maintaining eye contact, mimicking the baby's sounds and encouraging the baby to make more sounds are all central to working effectively with the younger sensorimotor infant.

    From 8 months onward (coordination of schemes) infants begin to show an understanding of certain words and will benefit from early years practitioners' commentaries on the various activities that are happening.

    Towards the end of the sensorimotor period, babies begin to vocalise more and more and communication is increasingly aided through the development of language. Early years practitioners can encourage movement in children's routine so that they can explore different areas of the environment and help them to name some of the objects they are encountering.

3. A lovely documentation of a project in Canada, which involved work with a small group of five children (an infant of 13 months, three toddlers and a preschooler) enrolled at a private day-care centre, brings home to us the pure and simple pleasures of the sensorimotor world for young children. The Canada Goose Project involved studying geese on nearby bodies of water over an extended period of time. In the following extract Brewer (2010, np) captures the pleasure and excitement of the experiences and provides a good illustration of the potential for working outdoors with very young children, still in the sensorimotor world.

    It is all about sensory experience. I believe that the noise and the wind and the sunlight dappling off the water are what draws the little ones to this place. I know it has drawn me since I was a child. For Lily, goose day is a delight for the senses: the wind on her face as it comes off the water, the sounds of the birds, the sunlight that she looks up at through squinted eyes. She enjoys the noises that the geese, gulls, and ducks make. I listen to her as she kind of honks like a goose. She found it much more fun to scream like the gulls. She smiles in delight at the gulls flying overhead and the cacophony of the geese clamouring around the picnic table. Infancy is such a wondrous time. She holds bread in her fists and eats it herself, not offering the geese any at all but enjoying their company.

4. According to Piaget, babies engage in intentional, purposeful behaviour in the fourth substage (coordination of schemes). Providing the young baby with an environment where there are safe opportunities to intentionally overcome simple obstacles can promote this development. Bradford provides an insightful illustration of how Ruby (10 months) is supported in overcoming the obstacle of reaching her teddy, which is sitting on a chair nearby:

> Ruby's key worker could go and get the teddy for her. Alternatively, Ruby may be able to reach it herself if her key worker walks her whilst holding both her hands. In this way Ruby's key worker provides assistance, her approach acting as a scaffold to Ruby's walking development. She talks to Ruby as she walks her along, saying 'Shall we go and get your teddy. Emma will walk with you, let's walk slowly . . .'
>
> (2012, p. 21)

5. Symbolic thought is one of the most profound developments in young children's cognitive development. As May (2011, p. 157) points out, children need external and visible reminders of the ideas they are coming to understand.

> Children need external props or concept maps such as counters, when learning to count, visual cues when learning to read, lots of practice playing with pouring water before the concept of the direction of water flow is established without doubt. In each area of the early years setting, therefore, we will see learning opportunities which are practical, progressive and available for long periods of time so that children can revisit and practice what they are coming to know.

6. While Piaget talked of universal stages in his theory, in order to guide the young infant's cognitive development it is essential to be attentive to the individual abilities and capacities of each infant, which can be challenging when there are a number of small babies needing care and attention. Treasure baskets, where the baby can reach for attractive objects and explore the various properties of these objects, are obviously an

appropriate resource for the young baby. However, it is important that the baby's natural desires to explore the room can be accommodated and the ordinary objects within the room are also available to the child.

Note

1. The concept of object permanence is briefly outlined here and detailed comprehensively in chapter 5.

Chapter 5

Object permanence
Out of sight, out of mind?

Objects are fascinating to children of all ages – curious to the smallest babies and a source of scientific wonder for older children, as illustrated in this passionately attentive observation of a 4-year-old girl by Mary Jane Drummond:

> A 4-year-old girl is looking at a collection of shells, rocks and pebbles untidily arranged on a table, with an assortment of magnifiers of different shapes and sizes. She selects one large spiral shell and examines it closely, first with the naked eye and then with some of the magnifiers. She uses the hand lenses, large and small, moving them to and fro to get the best magnification. She bends down and puts her face right up against the lens, as if she is trying to work out the best distance between her eyes, the lens and the shell. Then she puts the shell down on the table, placing it under a magnifying glass mounted on a tripod; she leans over the tripod, and looks intently at the shell, moving her head up and down, until she seems to be satisfied she has seen all there is to see. She picks up the shell again and holds it to each ear in turn. Then she puts the shell back on the table, under the tripod, and bends over it once more, laying her ear close to the lens, as is she were listening to the shell through the magnifying glass.
>
> (Drummond, 2010, p. 37)

This young child's meticulous attention to the detail of the shell she is exploring is a lovely example of how important it is to understand the unique properties of objects and their meaning in the world. By 4 years of age the child has developed many skills that help her to investigate these properties – the ability to seek out a particular shell, reach out and hold it and move it around in order to closely inspect its properties, the knowledge that if she bends towards the object she will be able to both see and hear its properties more intensely, and the knowledge that the magnifying glass will allow her to see the object right up close. What she has not yet quite grasped is that the magnifying glass will not allow her to hear the sounds any better than just placing it against her ear, but no doubt this knowledge is about to emerge with practice. Indeed the observation brings to mind the extraordinary and insightful detail that Piaget recorded when observing his own young children. The observation also conjures up Piaget's image of the child as the 'little scientist'.

In contrast to this 4-year-old girl, the very young sensorimotor infant, according to Piaget, is not aware of the presence of objects unless those objects are in sight. In this chapter we focus on how the young baby comes to an understanding of object permanence – the notion that when objects are out of sight they are not necessarily 'all gone'.

- Object permanence is Piaget's term for the child's understanding that objects continue to exist even when the individual is not perceptually aware of them.

So our focus is still very much on the sensorimotor world of the infant. Key messages from Piaget that we came away with in chapter 4 were:

- The sensorimotor infant – from birth to about 2 years – lives to a great extent in the *here-and-now*, a world where learning and development are largely facilitated through motor actions and sensory feedback.
- For the sensorimotor infant, until they reach approximately 8 or 9 months of age, if an object is not within sight, the young child appears to have no further knowledge of its existence.

Much research has been carried out since Piaget in order to further examine and update this knowledge about when and how babies understand the concept of object permanence. We will also summarise some more recent work on infants' knowledge about objects and the implications of this work. Why is an understanding of object permanence important for a child? What are the particular implications for professionals working with children in the early years? These questions we will try to address using some practical illustrations from early childhood experiences. And we will conclude by drawing together some reflections on how research on and knowledge about object permanence helps us support and plan for infant and toddler development in early years settings.

Why are we interested in understanding object permanence in infancy? What can object permanence tell us about other abilities at this very young age? In Piaget's description of infants' cognitive development, this understanding of the nature of objects has a very important place. Indeed, it is sometimes considered to be the major accomplishment of the first year of life, since understanding that objects have an independent, permanent existence is clearly essential for many aspects of life. Some implications of the development of this awareness are as follows:

- The importance of understanding object permanence for babies and children goes far beyond simply knowing that objects exist – it implies an ability to *represent in the mind* objects and people and to be able to retrieve or call up that mental representation when needed.
- If the child can represent an object, it is likely they can also represent people, in particular special people in their lives.
- When a child can understand and store the concept that an object/person continues to exist even when no longer visible, the child, or infant in this case, has the necessary tools for carrying out mental activities such as planning and prediction.

Objects can be people, plants, animals or just 'stuff', as Gopnik *et al.* (2001) point out. These authors go on to highlight the extent to which we take our ability to perceive and understand objects for granted. In order to illustrate this 'taking for granted' of our knowledge about objects and their properties, they bring to mind some of the strange and 'impossible' events we see in a magic show:

> Magicians make objects move from one point to another without traversing the space in between. The white rabbit was in the box and now it is in the top hat. They make what looks like one object into two objects: the single silver ring becomes two rings as we watch. They make objects seem to influence each other from a distance: the magician waves his magic wand and the box on the other side of the stage wiggles back and forth. They transform objects from one state to another: the water turns into orange juice. They even turn an inanimate object into a living one: the silk scarf becomes a dove.
>
> (Gopnik *et al.*, 2001, p. 61)

In fact, much of the research that built on Piaget's original experiments on object permanence has borrowed some of the strange events that we see performed by magicians in order to see if the young baby understands that the rules and expectations of physical reality are being violated or contested in some way. Understanding that objects are permanent and gaining insight into the precise features and properties of objects is considered one of the major milestones in the early years of a child's life (Bancroft & Flynn, 2005). The ability to represent objects, whether they are toy trains or people, is a critical skill that allows us to hold in mind a representation of the world in order to be able to reason about the environment (Bancroft & Flynn, 2005).

While working on Piaget's theory with early childhood education students, we asked them to observe young sensorimotor children's inter-actions with objects in their early years placement settings and to note episodes where the question of awareness of object permanence seemed to be relevant. Here are some examples of what these students observed in practice:

> When playing with Tanya (22 months) and small balls, I hid the balls and even though they were out of sight Tanya continued to look for where I was hiding them. Every time I put them in my pocket or under my leg, she went straight for them and pulled them out to her delight.

> While being fed Lizzie (8 months) throws her spoon on the floor and when I say 'spoon gone' – Lizzie looks at the floor and points to the spoon. I then give Lizzie a clean spoon but she continues to look at the spoon on the floor.
>
> When Kanji's (15 months) bottle is put in his basket, he knows it is still there because he walks over to the basket and waits for it to be given to him again.

> I am rolling a ball back and forth to Len (10 months), hiding it behind my back and Len smiles and puts his hands out because he wants me to roll the ball back to him.

> Catherine (14 months) was sitting down on the floor beside me. I was making notes in my diary – Catherine started to take an interest in my notebook and took it off me. Catherine started to turn pages and after a while I took the notebook back from her. I explained I needed to put it away. I put the notebook out of sight and almost immediately Catherine moved on to play with different toys.

Exploring object permanence with Piaget

How did Piaget explore this area? As with most of the constructs that Piaget investigated, the main targets of his observations were his own young children. In the extract overleaf, Piaget explores the understanding of object permanence in his young child Jacqueline.

From these and other observations, Piaget came to the conclusion that objects cease to exist for the young baby once they are no longer in sight – out of sight, out of mind! When Jacqueline's duck was hidden behind the fold of her sheet, she lost interest in it immediately.

Jacqueline tries to grasp a celluloid duck on top of her quilt. She almost catches it, shakes herself, and the duck slides down beside her. It falls very close to her hand but behind a fold in the sheet. Jacqueline's eyes have followed the movement, she has even followed it with her outstretched hand. But as soon as the duck has disappeared – nothing more! It does not occur to her to search behind the fold of the sheet, which would be very easy to do (she twists it mechanically without searching at all). But, curiously, she again begins to stir about as she did when trying to get the duck and again glances at the top of the quilt.

I then take the duck from its hiding place and place it near her hand three times. All three times she tries to grasp it, but when she is about to touch it I replace it very obviously under the sheet. Jacqueline immediately withdraws her hand and gives up. The second and third times I make her grasp the duck through the sheet and she shakes it for a brief moment but it does not occur to her to raise the cloth.

(Piaget, 1955, pp. 36–37)

What makes understanding object permanence difficult for infants?

By now we know that Piaget seemed to like complex terms when he was trying to describe his ideas! Let's meet two further terms, relevant to object permanence, that we will be coming back to several times in later chapters:

Centration – the tendency among young children to focus exclusively on just one aspect or feature of an activity or situation.
Egocentrism – young children are, to some extent, locked into their own worlds, unable to take the perspective of others.

Consider that if young infants are very much focused on what they perceive and how *they* perceive it, then it makes some sense to suggest that when they can no longer see an object, as far as they are concerned there *is* no longer an object (Oates *et al.*, 2005).

What helps infants understand object permanence?

As we move through this chapter, we will see that again the young child's emerging and increasing abilities to move around, reach out, touch, taste, hear, smell and to act on objects in the environment helps them to grasp the nature of the environment in which they are living. So, Piaget believed that infants gradually develop the knowledge that objects continue to exist even when they can no longer see them, and this knowledge is acquired as a result of their many chance explorations. For Piaget, at around 8 or 9 months of age, infants begin to look for objects that have disappeared – but this is only after many random trials, errors and varied experiences of events.

A game such as peek-a-boo, which is typically played with babies in the second half of their first year, is a fun way of learning that someone can 'disappear' behind a cloth and then 'reappear' (Robinson, 2011, p. 63). The author goes on to highlight a number of interesting aspects of the young child's behaviour, which link in with the development of an understanding of object permanence. Children begin to look for a dropped object, a behaviour that would not be typical for a younger child. Once they can move around, the young child begins to follow key people wherever they go, following a parent as they move around the house or a key worker as they move around a room in a setting and wanting to be close to that person. Object permanence is linked to attachment and proximity seeking. As Robinson (2011) further emphasises, the emergence of object permanence and the realisation that existence is permanent and continues even in absence is an awareness that needs to be further established and supported in practice with young children.

Between 8 and 12 months of age, Piaget suggested that infants achieve object permanence. Babies will now actively search for a hidden toy or similar object. For now, what is important is that the baby has progressed to being able to coordinate perceptual and motor behaviours and the mental representation of an object that is no longer in sight. Coordinating all these abilities allows the babies to search for an out-of-sight object and to understand that, if they continue to search, they will find the 'invisible' object.

It is interesting to consider that at a similar age (7–8 months) infants develop what is termed *clear-cut attachment*. In other words, their need for attention and physical comfort becomes focused on a very selective one or two attachment figures. We will return at the end of the chapter to highlight further links between the emergence of object permanence and changes in the child's behaviour that are associated with the development of skills such as 'social referencing' and the development of joint attention in young children.

More Piagetian tasks

Piaget's experiments also showed that searching for objects in this stage was still not without limitations. In what is known as the 'A not B error', once these young children have retrieved the object from a particular location, they will continue to search for the object in that *first* location, despite the fact that they have watched someone hide the object in a different location.

Over the next 6 months, the baby learns to retrieve hidden objects and no longer makes the A not B error. So, the baby has learned to mentally represent the object, mentally represent where the object is hidden and *combine* this knowledge with reaching out and moving or lifting whatever is now hiding the object. Piaget's findings on the development of understanding object permanence in infancy show that very early on the baby is developing cognitive abilities that allow it to access the meanings and features of objects in the world. But as we have seen above, the young infant's understanding of how things appear and disappear, where they are located and how they can be retrieved is very different from older children's and adults' understanding. DeHart *et al.* (2004) outline a further task designed to test knowledge about object permanence under more challenging conditions.

Show the baby a small object or toy – close your hand around the object while the child watches – place your hand under a cloth and with the baby watching, leave the object under the cloth and withdraw your hand. Babies tend to search for the object in your hand – and when they do not find the object, they may become upset or search randomly and finally uncover the object.

So while babies have now gained an understanding of the permanence of objects and of many of the essential properties of objects, they may not be able to make inferences about what happens to an object when it is not in sight.

A short extract from Gopnik *et al.* puts this in an amusing but insightful way:

For us it seems absolutely obvious that the keys must be under the cloth no matter how they're put there – where else could they be? But this is not only not obvious to the baby; it's something that has to be painstakingly learned. The baby, at first, lives in a perpetual magic show, where objects often seem to whirl about from one place to another with no rhyme or reason. Figuring out how it's all really done is one of the most important (Diamond, 1985) and difficult intellectual challenges of infancy.

(2001, p. 73)

Mother permanence vs object permanence

Piaget comes in for some criticism due to what has been considered his tendency to observe and try to understand the child in isolation from the significant others that inhabit the surrounding world. Piaget himself made reference to people permanence and believed that young babies were more likely to understand 'mother permanence' before they understood object permanence. Later theorists went on to test this hypothesis with mixed findings, but with some evidence of a *décalage* or *lag* in favour of mother over object permanence. Most recently, Slaughter and Boh (2001) explored whether infants between the ages of 7 and 14 months showed an awareness of mother permanence before object permanence. See below for some key points about this study and the findings:

- Infants were tested in two separate conditions in which they searched for their mothers and a large toy, both of which were hidden under curtained tables.
- The researchers used a delay period – they prevented the child from searching for the hidden object for increasing periods of time in order to assess how long the child could store the memory of the hidden mother or object.
- Infants were scored for the maximum delay that preceded a successful search.
- The results from 17 infants showed that there was a significant difference in length of time infants were able to hold on to mental representations, achieving greater success when searching for mothers as opposed to an attractive toy.

Before we move on to consider an update on Piaget's theory of the emergence of an understanding of object permanence, we are going to pause for a moment to reflect a little on and think about some of the implications that this ability has on practice in early childhood education.

Implications for practice

- For professionals working with babies, the understanding of object permanence is one of the earliest cognitive stages that is seen and is linked to growing memory. Games such as peek-a-boo and hiding objects help babies to practise this concept so that they begin to adapt to the many comings and goings of people in their world and to recognise that the person who goes will come back again (Robinson, 2011).
- As we have seen, early in infants' first year, they are becoming gradually more expert at gaining a more comprehensive understanding of physical objects, their properties and the physical laws associated with these. Babies represent physical events mentally and each representation builds on previous knowledge and experience. There are a number of simple games that babies and toddlers enjoy playing. Practitioners can support infants in their explorations and interactions with objects. Examples of

such games include building and knocking down stacks of simple objects. Practitioners can also model holding and dropping different objects with different outcomes – feathers float, soft toys flump, hard objects bang to the ground.

- An understanding of the permanence of objects in the world and the association with changes in the infant's behaviour parallel the emergence of very significant skills for the infant at this time. One of these is the profound attachment that infants are developing to the selected significant others in their lives, as their worlds become more stable and permanent. While many behaviours related to attachment to primary caregivers may occur within the home setting, early years practitioners play a major role in helping to build feelings of security and comfort in infants and in creating opportunities for shared interest and attention to develop and expand. May (2011) provides invaluable advice for early years professionals in highlighting the importance of grasping that babies of 10–11 months begin to show distress when their parent or carer leaves, as this developing concept of 'here or not here' leads to separation anxiety.
- Fun activities to build on understanding object permanence include simple peek-a-boo games, putting objects inside other objects and 'posting' objects – putting or allowing the baby to put a cork inside a glass bottle so that they can still see the object although it is now gone from their hands. Tassoni (2012) refers to these as 'enclosing games' and suggests that the benefits for young babies are both physical and cognitive.

From actions to expectations

In the 1980s a number of researchers, most notably Renee Baillargeon, University of Illinois, began to question some of the methods being used to investigate babies' awareness and understanding of object permanence. Some questions that these researchers asked were:

1. Did younger infants fail Piaget's object permanence tasks because they were unable to carry out necessary motor actions such as reaching out to grasp an object?
2. Did younger infants fail Piaget's object permanence tasks because they were unable to plan and carry out the actions necessary to retrieve the object?
3. Did younger infants fail Piaget's object permanence tasks because, although they might be able to plan and carry out actions necessary to retrieve the object, they were not yet able to simultaneously carry out these actions while mentally representing the objects?

In other words, were the demands of Piaget's tasks causing infants to fail to demonstrate their understanding of object permanence? More recent researchers have felt that perhaps Piaget was demanding too much of an infant to combine actions (reaching out and retrieving objects) and mental representations (storing in memory an image of the object). So, researchers played down the notion of infant actions by moving away from tasks that demanded that babies actually physically find objects. Instead, researchers explored children's apparent surprise at *impossible* events in attempts to establish whether they understood object permanence.

Baillargeon *et al.* (2011) describe three broad phases of work on object permanence since Piaget drew attention to this construct.

Phase 1: Focus shifted from exploring infant actions, such as finding an object, to infant *expectations* about objects.

Phase 2: Focused on *developmental patterns of success and failure* in infants' responses to physical events.

Phase 3: Final and ongoing phase has attempted to build a model of the *cognitive architecture* that makes this cognitive reasoning possible.

We will explore these three phases briefly, mindful that we cannot do justice to the wealth and detail of research that has been carried out in this area. Let's look at phase 1, where the emphasis was put on baby expectations about objects and their properties and possibilities. The Magic Show begins!

Magic show 1: Not what you expect! (Phase 1)

By magic event we mean something that appears to go against natural physical laws. Read through the two short vignettes below:

Normal event

A toy car runs down a ramp along a track and heads towards a large, solid block sitting in the middle of the track. The toy car heads straight for the block but as it cannot run through the block it is forced to stop before the block and can therefore not continue its journey along the track.

Magic event

A toy car runs down a ramp along a track and heads towards a large, solid block sitting in the middle of the track. The toy car heads straight for the block, disappears from sight, appears the other side of the block and continues to run along the track.

Solid objects (toy cars) cannot pass through other solid objects (block) unless a magician can make such an event happen. Before the show begins let's get to grips with some facts that will help us to understand how we can find out whether an infant of only a few months of age is surprised when such a 'magic' event happens.

- Fact 1: infants (and older children and adults) tend to look longer at objects or events that they perceive to be strange, new, novel or impossible (magic) rather than at familiar, possible or expected events.
- Fact 2: we can use this knowledge to develop observations where we can assess whether an infant judges an event to be unexpected or unfamiliar by timing how long they look at certain events – these tasks are called *violation of expectation (VOE)* tasks.

So, given that the toy car passing through the solid block is a violation of our expectations, we would expect the young baby to experience that event as unexpected and therefore to look at it longer than at a normal event.

Some of the first magic shows were devised by Renee Baillargeon, professor of psychology at the University of Illinois Urbana-Champaign, whose work focuses on the development of cognition in infancy. Baillargeon, building on the work of Piaget and others before her, has been carrying out research on infant knowledge of objects, with a particular focus on infants' construction of knowledge about hidden objects. Her findings have confirmed that Piaget underestimated the infant's competence in this area. Two key messages have emerged from her many years of work in this area:

1. Even very young infants of 2½ months possess expectations about physical events – we will explore and illustrate this further in this section.
2. Infants' expectations about physical events develop in a very systematic and predictable manner in the first year of their lives – we will explore and illustrate this further in the following section.

How do we know that young infants have certain expectations about the physical properties of the world? In one situation, an expected event takes place, while in the other situation an unexpected event takes place – infants are observed and the length of time they look at each event is recorded and compared. A nice example of such a task is outlined below.

What we expect to find in the infant's responses to such 'magic' events is an element of surprise in their response. Although their expression may not communicate 'what's going on here?!!', what we will notice is a heightened state of attention to the strange event – if the baby detects the magic event – that is a violation of natural physical laws.

The disappearing train (Bower et al., 1971)

Children of about 2 months of age were positioned in such a way that they could see a toy train moving from one end of a length of track to the other, passing behind a screen placed half-way along the route. Part of the procedure involved stopping the train behind the screen and when that happened the direction of the child's gaze was recorded. If the child had no understanding that the train continued to exist when it was behind the screen then there should be no specific direction for his or her gaze. However, if the infant did understand that the train continued to exist when it was behind the screen, it was predicted that their gaze should follow along the direction of the track, as they would expect the train to emerge from the screen. With respect to Piaget's findings, the results were surprising. Once the train had disappeared behind the screen, the children looked at the part of the track that it would have reached had it not stopped. Children of only 2 months would follow the progress of the train and appear to anticipate its reappearance from behind the screen. In a variation of this procedure, children were shown one object disappearing behind the screen and a different object appearing from the other side. In this case, their pattern of gaze did not follow the path smoothly but was apparently disrupted by the appearance of the new object.

Magic show 2: Bit by bit, category by category (phase 2)

Spurred on by the discovery that very young infants recognise magic events, researchers moved to find out more detail about:

1. How knowledge about magic events emerges across the different stages of infancy.
2. Whether there are *kinds of knowledge* associated with *different categories of objects* and what these patterns might be.

Some very interesting findings emerged in these studies. Before we briefly review some of these findings and think about the implications, let's take a minute to reflect on some more terms in order to understand the kind of research that was carried out. Different ways of hiding objects were used and involve an understanding of the following terms:

Occlusion: an obstruction that may prevent you from seeing something, for example a small child may be hidden from view behind a wall.
Containment: something may be hidden because it is inside something else; it is contained within a box, for example.

Covering: something may be hidden because you put a cover over it; the washcloth over the keys is a good example.

What researchers have found is that knowledge about magic events and the consequent surprise generated by these events develops in sequence across different ages in infancy. Surprisingly though, *when* that knowledge emerges depends on the *kind* of 'event category' that is being represented – so whether an object is being hidden by some kind of screen (occlusion), hidden or contained within a box (containment), or hidden when covered by something from top down (covering) – babies seem to learn about the rules of these events at *different times* and *in a particular sequence*.

Development within event categories

Let's take a few examples beginning with what is termed *occlusion events*.

- At 2½ months an infant, as indeed an adult, is surprised if a mouse is not visible when moving from A to B to C (Figure 5.1).

But look at the next magic event! The mouse passes through an open space where he appears to disappear, yet appears the other side of the open space.

- The 2½-month-old infant is *not* surprised at this magic event, but the 3-month-old infant is surprised – but *only* if the *top* edge of the occlusion or obstruction is continuous or connected (not the bottom edge) (Figure 5.2).
- By 3½ months the infant is also surprised if the *bottom* edge of the occlusion or obstruction is continuous or connected (Figure 5.3).

What these strange experiments seem to be telling us is that:

- Very young infants, at 2½ months, can mentally represent the mouse (while the mouse is hidden behind the columns).

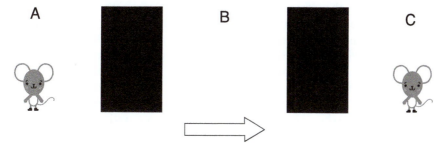

Figure 5.1. Impossible event: discontinuous occlusion

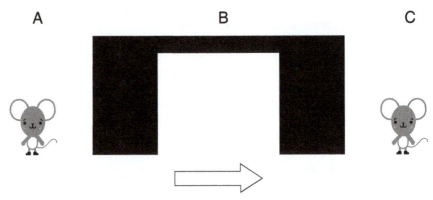

Figure 5.2. Impossible event: occlusion continuous at top edge

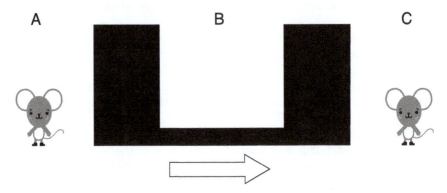

Figure 5.3. Impossible event: occlusion continuous at bottom edge

- Knowledge and consequent expectations about physical rules/laws seem to build incrementally so that over time the infant attends to more and more detailed information (e.g. relative *height* of tall objects and whether they should be visible or not behind a short occluder).

So, knowledge about hidden objects and the natural physical rules involved is developing as the infant is getting a little older. No great surprise there . . . but what is the most important fact to remember here is that Piaget believed that infants cannot mentally represent objects until at least the end of their first year, whereas these young babies at 2½ months are able to mentally represent the image of the mouse when it is hidden behind the screen. Furthermore, they expect to be able to see the mouse when it is walking in the opening between the two screens. And the extent to which they expect to see the mouse when the occluders are continuous varies depending on whether they are joined at the top or bottom!

Similar to Piaget's schema system, which becomes more and more complex and sophisticated with experience, Baillargeon and her many colleagues propose that babies develop what they call a 'knowledge tree', which expands in terms of the branches of knowledge available to them. Through experience they develop what are termed *vectors* – rules about what variables or details to pay attention to – height, width, transparency and so on.

One of the strangest findings of these experiments is that, for example, knowledge about height and occlusion seems to develop earlier than, for example, height in containment, which in turn develops earlier than knowledge about height when an object is covered from the top downwards.

Development across event categories

Researchers went on to find out if knowledge about physical laws and their associated expectations developed differently when it involved different events – for example, would the infant react differently to seeing a tall teddy hidden behind a small wall as opposed, for example, to seeing a tall teddy hidden inside a closed container? And the answer is yes – infants seem to recognise these violations at different ages. Some of these décalages are summarised below:

- By 4½ months infants are surprised if a tall object is hidden behind a short occluder, but it is not until infants are 7 months old that they are surprised if a tall object is hidden within a short container.
- Infants can only detect violation when a tall object is hidden when covered with a shorter cover when they get to 12 months of age.

Explaining the magic (phase 3)

We will now summarise and integrate some of the findings that have emerged over recent years with regard to infant reasoning about objects and the physical world. For example, how can we understand why very young infants successfully detect certain violations and older infants fail to detect other violations? Some of the things that that we have learned since Piaget are:

- Infants identify event categories.
- Infants identify vectors or rules associated with these event categories.
- From these vectors they develop a sequence of variables that allow them to predict expected and unexpected events.
- Infants do not generalise information from one event category to another.

Baillargeon and her colleagues have been working to build a model that can help us understand how the young baby builds up knowledge about what is happening in the physical world. She calls this a *physical reasoning system* that is dedicated to monitoring events as they unfold and interpreting their outcomes. So, for example, when infants watch a physical event, they build a physical representation of the event that they subsequently use to interpret and predict future events.

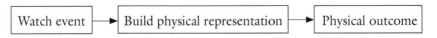

All the information included in these physical representations will become subject to core principles and these core principles are innate – in other words babies are born with these principles (Baillargeon *et al.*, 2011).

During their first few weeks in the world, infants' physical representations are very basic to include fundamental spatial and temporal knowledge. So while the infant may understand that if an object is in a container it should not be visible – the essence of the event – many of the details of the event are not included in this representation. Details such as the relative height and width of the object compared to the occluder or container are not available to the very young infant, which explains some of the findings above.

As we conclude this chapter, let's try to summarise the main elements of Baillargeon's model of infant physical reasoning.

1.   Very young infants understand *basic continuity variables* – put a cover over an object and the object disappears. Take the cover off the object and the object reappears. Basic continuity variables are typically detected early because they only involve basic information that young infants represent about events.
2.   Older infants develop an understanding of *variable continuity violations* that are typically detected only after infants have identified the key variables as relevant for the event categories involved – e.g. the relative height of the objects in relation to the occluder, the relative width of the object in relation to the container and so on.

Implications for practice

We have already summarised some of the implications for practice of the young sensorimotor infant's growing ability to understand object permanence. Since Piaget, we have seen that there has been a very substantial amount of work that has continued to explore object permanence abilities and that suggests that infants can mentally represent objects at a much earlier age and stage than Piaget suggested. Below we reflect further on some of the possible implications that arise from what we have learned about babies and their understanding of the permanence of objects in their worlds.

- The importance of providing opportunities for 'trial and error' learning is emphasised again in recent research on object permanence. Baillargeon uses the metaphor of 'whispering in the baby's ear' to describe the ways in which we can 'prompt' babies to pay attention to details in the events that they are experiencing. Using playful and fun activities with objects, the baby's primitive physical reasoning system can be expanded. By the time they are 1 year old, babies, like little scientists, will systematically test out and vary the actions they perform on objects. These explorations can be promoted through the provision of safe resources that the baby can explore.

- The game of peek-a-boo, with its links with something being there when out of sight – and being the same object – and with fun and shared experience, is one that often attracts babies from their object play and provides, through this simple procedure, a link between emotions and the learning of concepts.

- The joy of exploration of objects and the growing understanding of object permanence in infancy can be supported by early childhood practitioners through encouraging 'shared attention' to objects. With the incremental advances in understanding objects, their properties, the categories they belong to and the fact that they are permanent, the baby has access to a sharing and linking of minds. This new ability to invite others to share responses to events and objects allows greater connection with the world and greater awareness of being an individual.

- Smidt (2011) draws attention to the concept of *object highlighting*, developed by Bruner. Two examples that can be applied to the early years setting involve picking up an object and vocalising in a high toned voice (for example, 'look at this gorgeous little teddy!') to draw the child's attention. Another example is where an adult picks up an object that the baby is focusing on and draws it into the space between the baby and themselves, again vocalising and inviting the baby to share their attention and interest in the object.

Chapter 6

The preoperational world

Symbolic function substage

By 2 years of age children 'look beyond the superficial features of the object to try to determine the deeper laws that govern what the object will do' (Gopnik *et al.*, 2001, p. 83). In the sensorimotor stage, we saw that babies find magic events[1] interesting, and consequently tend to stare longer at such events. Now, however, the preoperational child's response to magic events is to seek logical explanations for why and how things happen. They have moved to a more in-depth analysis of the world and begin to look for logical and reasonable answers to explain some of the magic happening in the world around them. Let's compare the learning style of a child in Piaget's sensorimotor stage of cognitive development with children who are a little older and within Piaget's preoperational stage.

> Lee (1 year, 7 months) sits in the construction area in his day-care setting, exploring the different possibilities of fitting small blocks into larger blocks. 'Will we try the blue one, Lee – can we fit the blue one into the big red block here?' prompts Jill, his key worker. Lee tries to fit the blue block into the red block and when it slips in he smiles and picks up another block. Gradually, as he practises in a trial and error way, he accommodates new knowledge into his schema for fitting. Small blocks fit inside big blocks.

Lee is still in the sensorimotor world where his learning is mostly through acting on the concrete world of objects. Actions and observations lead him to the knowledge that small fits inside big – and eventually he adapts his schema for fitting things according to his observations.

The children in the following extract are between 3 and 5 years of age, all within Piaget's preoperational stage of cognitive development. Spencer and Hall (2010) document findings from a project where the children worked together to investigate and make representations of elements of an underwater environment. In this extract, the children are discussing how to design tails for mermaid costumes:

OLIVIA:	What if we invent something that is straight so we can walk?
TEACHER:	Do mermaids walk?
GROUP:	No!
TEACHER:	How then do mermaids move?
MARY:	They swim.
MORGAN:	What if they walked on their tails?
OLIVIA:	They would be standing on their tippy toes.
MARY:	I was talking about we need our legs together and something to hold their feet together.
MADDY:	On your feet, the tails will stick together so your feet need to be together.
MCKENZIE:	Mermaids can touch their nose with their tails.
ZEN ROSE:	A tail goes from here to there (pointing to toes and hip, respectively).

Here, the children work together to question and find answers to some of the challenges involved in making tails for mermaids. The children use language and talk together to explore information and knowledge and their approaches to problem solving were enhanced through collaboration (Spencer & Hall, 2010). They accommodate new knowledge about size and shape and the consequences of these for mermaids being able to walk.

Piaget's use of the word 'operations' within his theory of cognitive development refers to the internalised set of actions that enable children to do *mentally* those things that before they had done *physically*. So, while the sensorimotor child acts physically on objects and internalises the knowledge that results from these actions, the preoperational child's thinking is progressing and beginning to add a dimension to their experiences – a dimension that allows them to think about and even imagine acting on objects. Another name for this Piagetian stage is pre-conceptual, which means that the child's thinking is still quite reliant on the physical world around them and they are just beginning to form concepts about their environment.

Our aim in this chapter is to identify key milestones and cognitive achievements within this stage, and to clarify and illustrate these through concrete examples from children's experiences in preschool settings and more broadly in the real world. During this preoperational stage children's mental grasp of the world gradually becomes more complex and, at the same time, more efficient in representing the world around them. Many of the abilities that we have seen emerging in the sensorimotor stage up to 2 years of age now become more refined during the 3rd year and onwards. Symbolic thought and journeys into the fantasy world of pretend play also characterise these preoperational years.

Within this preoperational stage, Piaget identified two further two substages:

- Symbolic function substage (approximately 2–4 years of age).
- Intuitive thought substage (approximately 4–7 years of age).

In this chapter we are focusing on the first of these substages. It is important to highlight that many of Piaget's findings on children's abilities in this pre-operational stage have been revised and updated. However, significantly Piaget set the agenda for so much of the fascinating research that would follow on from his theory and that would help us to gain insight into the knowledge we have today about children's cognitive development and abilities.

Symbolic function substage (2–4 years)

Before we begin to outline some of the principles in these substages, it is useful to unpack some challenging terms in order to be able to better understand some of the concepts that Piaget was drawing attention to. We have come across the term 'symbolic' several times in previous chapters. As we have seen, symbolic thought is the ability to let one thing stand for another, as for example, a child who uses a building block to represent a smartphone. So when Piaget named this period in childhood cognitive development the symbolic function substage, he wanted to emphasise the child's growing ability to use things such as images, words and gestures to *represent* objects and events in the world. Within the first of these substages, children increasingly use symbols such as scribbling, drawing, using language, engaging in pretend play, and all of these abilities are supported and enhanced through activities in preschool settings.

Below are some observations recorded in early childhood settings by students of early childhood education, which give us some insight into key features of the child's preoperational world. All of these children are in the first stage of Piaget's preoperational stage of development.

> Carrie (2 years, 5 months) is in the home corner playing with her baby doll and pretending to cook for 'baby' and feed her. She carefully puts 'baby' to bed and pulls the covers up to keep 'baby' warm. Throughout her play Carrie talks to herself and the 'baby'. Carrie plays alone with no interaction with other children.

Every morning the children (aged 3–4 years) in my room play a game where they crawl on the floor and bark as they are pretending to be dogs. This game goes on for quite some time with different children taking on the roles of different dogs.

The children (2 years, 5 months to 3 years, 5 months) play in the magic room, an area designed for play in the crèche. Chris (3 years, 5 months) plays in the kitchen corner. He is busy pretending to make dinner. He hands me a cup and says 'That's your tea!' I thank him and he says 'Dinner will be ready soon'.

Tommy (2 years, 8 months) draws some squiggles on a page in different colours. I ask him if he wants to tell me what he has drawn. He tells me that the pink scribble is mummy, the blue scribble is daddy and the red scribble is Lightning McQueen!

These simple observations tell us so much about what is happening in the early stages of the preoperational world. The magic continues into this world but this time the child *makes magic happen* and explores the great pleasures of the world of the imagination.

Three key elements of cognitive development are highlighted within this substage:

Symbolic representation: the ability to make one thing stand for another – for example, a small tin box may stand for a smartphone.

Egocentrism: the tendency for children to see things only from their own perspective and to lack the ability to see things from the perspective of others.

Animism: the tendency to attribute human lifelike qualities to inanimate objects – for example, a door might be 'a bold door' because it slammed shut in the wind.

Symbolic representation

The ability to think symbolically and to represent the world mentally predominates in this early substage of preoperational thought. Changes in the nature of representation according to children's age and stage of development was a central tenet of Piaget's theory (Schaffer, 2006). Smidt (in Allery, 2010) emphasises the significance of the emergence of symbolic representation as follows:

> The ability to make one thing stand for another is crucial in early learning. We live in a highly symbolic world. The words we speak, the texts we read, the images we see, the logos we encounter, the numbers we use are all symbols. In order to be able to move away from the here and now and into the abstract world of letters, numbers and symbols, young children need to explore symbolic representation through their play.
>
> (2010, p. 35)

While we have seen in chapter 5 that Piaget underestimated the ability of the young infant to use symbolic representation, he was accurate in highlighting that from the age of 2 years onwards, with the emergence and support of language, the child moves away from an exclusive reliance on sensorimotor stimuli and the concrete world, to a much more expansive experience within the world of symbols and imagination.

Emily (2 years, 8 months) has a rectangular-shaped tin box clasped to her ear and is speaking loudly into this box, which has become a mobile phone for her. Completely absorbed, she babbles continuously, raising her voice to be heard, most likely in imitation of adults she has observed doing likewise.

In this instance, the tin box represents a mobile phone for Emily. In this first stage of the preoperational world, children use many different types of symbols and what is most important is the meaning and significance that the child attaches to the object.

Symbolic play

Piaget defined three stages and categories of play. The second category of play, *symbolic play*, involved the use of mental representations and included pretend, fantasy and socio-dramatic play. This kind of play was believed to be evident in children between 2 and 6 years of age, roughly corresponding to the preoperational stage of cognitive development. As previously outlined, it is important to point out that Piaget himself did not place great emphasis on play as a primary means of learning but rather as an activity that supported learning (Wood & Atfield, 2005). According to Piaget, play promoted assimilation rather than accommodation and therefore consolidated newly learned behaviours and actions.

Schaffer (2006) points out children use a variety of symbols to represent objects and people in the world. Some symbols can be idiosyncratic – not immediately obvious to the onlooker: a piece of wood can become an express train whizzing down the tracks, a spoon can become the gate through which the farmer must pass in order to feed his animals, a tissue can become the tiny baby's bedclothes, tenderly tucked in to keep her warm. Other types of symbols, such as pictures, maps and models, are more obviously representations. In the following section we will look at the most important form of representation – words as symbols representing objects. While symbols may differ in type, they share the feature that they are used to denote something other than themselves. Vygotsky, who followed Piaget, highlighted the importance of *internalisation* – the means by which symbols are mentally represented through language and are therefore an effective and efficient way of storing experiences in memory, which can be drawn on to look back on the past and to anticipate the future (Schaffer, 2006).

So, while Piaget used the term 'symbolic representation' to signpost the child's progression towards the ability to make meaning through symbols, Vygotsky went on to develop his theory of cognitive development, expanding on the area of symbolic representation. Smidt (2009) highlights two important constructs that Vygotsky developed in his theory of cognitive development.

- Decontextualisation of meaning: the ability the child develops to think about something even when the thing is not present or evident.

Let's think for a moment in Piagetian terms about what this means. In the early stages of the sensorimotor world, objects seemed to fade from existence if they were not in sight. The cognitive abilities of the child are now advancing to a point where not only do they not need objects to be present in order to believe in their existence, *but they can now actually pretend that objects are present when in fact they are not.*

- Rule: any pretend play situation involves a rule if we define 'rule' as a specific principle to which the child adjusts. Moreover, this rule develops through the child's active experience of the object and the consequent meaning that the child has attributed to the object.

Let's go play for a few minutes and see if we can identify these two constructs in children playing in their preoperational worlds.

> Jeannie (4 years old) wants to be a mermaid so she puts on a greeny/blue dress and pretends to be swimming along the floor.

> Ruby and Alice (both 2 years, 8 months) are playing hairdressers – they use the musical instruments (rice in bottles) to be the shampoo and a pretend spoon to be the brush.

> Jessica (2 years) engages in pretend play with the encouragement of Karen (early childhood education practitioner). Jessica pretends to have her 'wand' and says 'abra kadabra . . . a cat!' Karen responds by immediately behaving like a cat. Jessica continues this scenario with many different animals.

> Robert (3 years, 5 months), makes siren noises and pretends to be a policeman.

We can see that as these children play, they use objects to create and sustain their fantasies. As children move through the symbolic function substage of Piaget's preoperational world, they become better able to create and sustain fantasy without props and their dramatic enactments are often enriched with language. In the final observation above, the child is no longer reliant on props to sustain his fantasy but can imagine himself as a policeman through imitations and vocalisations.

Language as symbols

When we think of the 2-year-old child in early childhood settings, one of the major accomplishments that springs to mind is the rapid acquisition of language. For Piaget, it is the child's development of the symbol function that enables them to acquire language proficiency so quickly. Again, in the short observation below we can see the gradual progression in the child's cognitive ability to combine symbolic representation visually and through language.

> Max (3 years, 7 months) draws a red picture of love hearts and says it is for Valentine's day and for his Mam. He is able to recognise that hearts can symbolise Valentine's day and tells me about it.

The symbolic process in language is also apparent in imaginative play and we have seen as the child progresses through this preoperational stage, fantasy is sustained through movement and vocalisation and without the need for props.

> Lucy (3 years, 9 months) and Sarah (3 years, 5 months) love playing in the house area. One of their favourite scenes to play is pretending they are two mothers and protecting their children from a monster. They use sounds such as 'roar' to represent the monster. They call the police using their phones. Their language is clear and articulate.

Once the child begins to use language symbols, they broaden their problem-solving abilities greatly and begin to learn from the verbalisations of others. Whitebread (2012) draws attention to the phenomenon of 'private speech', identified by Piaget and Vygotsky, which was believed to allow the child to monitor and regulate the goals and progression of an activity and to be particularly associated with object and construction play.

> Simon (3 years, 9 months) is engrossed in making a jigsaw and talks to himself as he works through the puzzle, saying 'This piece doesn't go there . . . this piece isn't for the jigsaw'.

> Circle time – all children sit and participate in the conversation. Julie asks Malcolm (3 years, 9 months) what he did over the weekend. He explains Saturday and Sunday are his days off and carefully describes his visit to the park. He is constructing long sentences.

We can see that Piaget's symbolic function substage pays great attention to the development of the fascinating ability to use a simple object and activity to represent something more complex. This understanding of the concept of symbolism develops alongside the development of language, which the child uses in order to find words to accompany their play experiences and their rehearsal of adult roles. An important reminder that symbolic thought is not a concept to be rushed is provided by May (2011) when she states that young children need external and visible reminders of the ideas they are grappling with. Learning opportunities within each area of the early years setting should be progressive and available to children over long periods of time so that they can revisit, review and practice what they are coming to know.

Let's conclude this section with a lovely illustration of a curriculum in action that offers the child endless opportunities and potential for expression through symbolic representation. Pope-Edwards (2002, np) provides a rich and insightful portrait of the Reggio Emilio approach to early childhood education in action in the following extract:

> Children grow in competence to symbolically represent ideas and feelings through any of their 'hundreds of languages' (expressive, communicative, and cognitive) – words, movement, drawing, painting, building, sculpture, shadow play, collage, dramatic play, music, to name a few – that they systemically explore and combine. Teachers follow the children's interests and do not provide focused instruction in reading and writing; however, they foster emergent literacy as children record and manipulate their ideas and communicate with others. The curriculum has purposive progression but not scope and sequence. Teaching and learning are negotiated, emergent processes between adults and children, involving generous time and in-depth revisiting and reviewing. Close, multiyear adult–child and peer relations are fostered, usually through a looping organization. Long-term, open-ended projects are important vehicles for collaborative work, in classroom environments carefully prepared to offer complexity, beauty, and a sense of well-being and ease.

Egocentrism

When we think of the word 'egocentric' it tends to conjure up the idea of selfishness. However, when Piaget used this term, his emphasis was on the child's tendency to perceive the world solely from their own perspective and to be unaware that other people may have different perspectives (Schaffer, 2006).

In chapter 5 we came across the term 'centration', which we explained as the young child's tendency to focus on only one feature of an object or a situation at a time, to the exclusion of all other potentially relevant features. An example of centration is illustrated below:

> Mark (3 years, 7 months) is doing a jigsaw puzzle while Julie observes him. He is looking for a piece to complete the sky in the scene, which is blue and cloudless. While trying to find a suitable piece to fit, he focuses only on finding a piece with blue on it. He is centring on colour as the feature that will unlock the key to finding the missing piece. What he is not focusing on is the shape of the piece. So for now, he has to go through all the steps of fitting every blue piece to the puzzle until he finds the one that fits.

Schaffer (2006) compares the egocentrism of the young child's account of a story that focuses on very recent events and assumes a shared knowledge about experiences that are not common. Young children take for granted that knowledge already exists and this may be due to the fact that up to 3–4 years of age, the young child cannot clearly grasp the idea that there are clear boundaries between their minds and the minds of those they are interacting with. We will come back to this in more detail in chapter 7 and look at some fascinating work that has been carried out with children under the broad term 'theory of mind' abilities. For now, we will highlight briefly key aspects of egocentrism as conceptualised by Piaget (1929).

Perceptual egocentrism

Piaget observed that young children assume that other people see things from the same perspective as they do, even if they are facing in the opposite direction and have a different view in front of them. One of the most famous tasks that Piaget devised was known as the Three Mountain Task (Piaget & Inhelder, 1956). Based on findings from this task, Piaget concluded that children continue to see things from their own perspective right through the preoperational period and until they are approximately 7 years of age. See a full description of this experiment in chapter 7.

However, there have been many criticisms of Piaget's Three Mountain Task. Donaldson (1978) revised Piaget's task to make it more meaningful to young children and found that 90% of the responses of children aged between 3½ and 5 years were correct. We will review some of the more recent research on children's ability to take the perspective of others in the following chapter.

Another form of egocentrism in childhood that Piaget drew attention to is *communicative egocentrism*, where children talk to themselves or engage in dialogue with someone else but are not mindful of the fact that the other person does not have access to the same information as they do. A very good illustration of this is the child in conversation with her Dad on the phone, who, when he asks if her mummy is there – replies by nodding. The child does not take on board the fact that her father cannot see her and so believes that she can communicate through gestures as she would if her Dad were present.

During this symbolic function substage, children also believe that moral rules depend solely on the authority of their own parents, whose rules must be adhered to regardless of the circumstances or particular context in which they occur. As children move through the preoperational world they become more aware of the need for mutual negotiation and reciprocity. We will return to the concept of egocentrism in early childhood in chapter 7 and spend more time clarifying and illustrating some of the implications of Piaget's ideas on egocentrism.

Animism

How often have we consoled the young child who tumbles to the ground having fallen over teddy by picking up teddy and saying 'Silly teddy for getting in Clare's way – Teddy will have to be more careful so Clare does not fall again!'? As adults we are responding to the young child's animism – their belief that objects are alive and have lifelike features and qualities.

Here is an extract from some of Piaget's work in which Piaget is in conversation with a preoperational child:

PIAGET: Does the sun move?
CHILD: Yes, when one walks it follows. When one turns around, it turns around too. Doesn't it ever follow you too?
PIAGET: Why does it move?
CHILD: Because when one walks, it goes too.
PIAGET: Why does it go?
CHILD: To hear what we say.
PIAGET: Is it alive?
CHILD: Of course, otherwise it wouldn't follow us, it couldn't shine.

(Piaget, 1960, p. 215)

In this short extract we can see that from the child's point of view, their existence is determining what happens in the world around them – things have to be able to move, hear and see so that they can move in parallel with the child, illustrated by the fact the child believes that the sun could not shine if it did not follow him/her.

Update on symbolic function substage

What we know now about symbolic thinking

While Piaget did not argue for the leading role that play can have in learning, Vygotsky went on to argue that play makes a significant contribution to the development of symbolic representation such as drawing and other forms of visual art, language, mathematical symbols systems and so on (Whitebread, 2012). In Vygotskian terms, pretend play allows a transition from the purely situational constraints of early childhood to the adult capability for abstract thought. When children have a new and interesting experience, they assimilate this experience by *acting out* significant events, rather than thinking about it. The following extract provides a lovely illustration of moving through this transition:

> Sarah (1 year old) was clearly beginning to use sounds (not yet quite words!) to carry meaning ('Mama', 'Dada', etc.). She was also, as it

happened, playing quite a lot with a particular peg doll. I had watched her 'exploring' this doll as an object on a number of occasions. She looked at it while she wiggled it about, turned it upside-down, dropped it and picked it up. She put it to her mouth, waved it about vigorously and banged it against other objects. Then, one morning, there was a new development. Sarah made the doll move as though walking along and made little humming noises as she did so. Suddenly, the peg doll was not just an object, she was a pretend little person, a symbol.

(Whitebread, 2012, p. 66)

Children can act out their representations in many ways apart from symbolic play as, for example, through drawing and painting and through musical play.

Vygotsky's claim for the support of pretend play and the emergence of representational thought and language seem to be well supported in this illustration and a number of studies would support this link. However, other researchers argue that there is no clear evidence for play being instrumental in facilitating cognitive outcomes, rather it is believed that it has a supportive role (Lillard *et al.*, 2012).

In contrast to Vygotsky, Jerome Bruner believed that the child goes through three stages of representational thought:

Enactive stage: Children develop understanding through action on objects.
Iconic stage: Children are able to make mental images and do not need to have the physical presence of an object.
Symbolic stage: Children use abstract ideas to represent the world, to evaluate it and think critically about it.

Piaget's categories of play have also been challenged. We know now that play cannot be neatly classified into three categories and that there is a substantial amount of overlap between the different types of play. While Piaget believed that symbolic play is evident from 2 years of age, and while we know that children spend much of their time in fantasy activities in play between 2 and 5 years of age, we also know that young children engage in simple forms of symbolic play before they are 2 years of age.

What we know now about egocentrism

Several criticisms have been levelled at Piaget's claims about the abilities of the child in this symbolic function substage of their preoperational worlds. First of all, the Three Mountain Task has been viewed as somewhat meaningless and irrelevant to a young child who may have little experience of mountains, let alone mountains from different perspectives. More recently, researchers have carried out tasks with young children that try to use more meaningful materials. For example, when researchers used layouts of toys that young children typically play with in order to investigate their knowledge about the perspective of other people, children as young as 3 or 4 years of age had some understanding of how another person looking at the layout might see it (Smith *et al.*, 2003). In more meaningful and child-friendly designed tasks, Margaret Donaldson and other researchers have shown that young children have the ability to take the perspective of another person at an earlier age than Piaget suggested. Whitebread (2012) draws our attention to the large body of post-Piagetian theory of mind research that has identified children's ability to attribute states of mind to other people, quite distinct from their own state of mind, between the ages of 3 and 4 years.

What we know now about animism

Piaget's tasks illustrating the child's belief in animism have been criticised. For example, the sun, the moon and the stars are somewhat inaccessible 'objects' to all of us – and it is not uncommon for even adults to attribute a certain human or even superhuman power to these elements of our universe. More recent research on children's understanding of animism indicates that children understand and can make quite clear distinctions between living and non-living things at a much earlier age than Piaget proposed. Opfer and Gelman (2011) draw attention to the fact that the first signs of the person–object distinction appear much earlier than at 8 months as Piaget (1952) had indicated.

Implications for practice

What are the implications of Piaget's first substage of the preoperational world for practitioners working with children in early years settings? The ability to suspend reality and to be able to use one thing in order to represent something else is a very significant development within these early preoperational years. May (2011) points out that symbolism runs through our lives at many levels – in writing, paintings, maths and drama. One of the most significant activities that children engage in during this early preoperational stage is that of pretend play – using symbols to represent objects and activities. Young children engage in role play and through these fun activities rehearse and try out experiences that are not yet possible in their actual lives, but that allow them to gain knowledge and experience in terms of generating ideas, practising and expanding on language and communication skills, learning to negotiate, cooperate and take turns where appropriate, and learning about the feelings and intentions of others in their play activities.

- Symbols are everywhere in our world and Piaget, through his use of the term 'symbolic function substage', highlighted the emergence of these abilities in the young child. As we have seen, children express themselves through symbols in a number of ways, in their play, their drawings and paintings, through dance and music. Whitebread (2012) draws attention to the development of a 'graphic grammar' that enables children to represent symbolically their meanings through visual images. Young preoperational children and, to a lesser extent, children in the sensorimotor stage, like to leave their mark on surfaces that they come into contact with. Mark-making for the very young preoperational child may need more guidance from adults, but toddlers can still make choices about where and how to draw (May, 2011). As emphasised by many authors, it is the process rather than the end-product that is central to learning.

- Children's enjoyment and excitement in taking part in expressive activities can be supported through the provision of resources for symbolic representation through splatter painting and making marks with fingers or with feet (May, 2011). There are endless possibilities in terms of printing with a variety of objects, making marks in dough and wet sand and other materials. May (2011) draws attention to an international early years conference held in Reggio Emilia in 2004 that was called 'Traces of Identity'. One of the aims of the conference was to explore the basic need that even a very young child has to make an impression on their world and to leave a trace of who they are as evidence of their value and individuality.

- The adult role in supporting symbolic representation is key and while Piaget did not elaborate on the adult role, his theories around the very young child's simple but emerging ability to represent the world symbolically provide guidance in terms of how we can best support children of different ages in their fantasy roles. For younger children, from 2 to 3 years of age, whose symbolic representation is still somewhat constrained by their reliance on external props to support it, it may be beneficial to arrange a separate area for their fantasy activities, which are likely to be less well developed in terms of plot. Younger children may benefit from having an adult present to stimulate and support the extension of their simple pretend scenarios. Early years professionals can encourage and support the young preoperational child in providing opportunities for children to think and talk about possible role-play scenarios that can be designed to develop and expand over a number of days. Children can be provided with many opportunities to practise being in certain roles before they actually take on these roles in their drama.

- The concept of *sustained shared thinking* is relevant to development in this first substage of Piaget's preoperational world. Sustained shared thinking can be described as 'thinking together to build meaning and understanding' (NCCA, 2009). One of the principles emphasised in *Aistear: The Early Childhood Curriculum Framework* in Ireland highlights the importance and benefits for young children of promoting early childhood practitioners and children talking and thinking together. A lovely illustration of this is provided in the following extract:

'See it got stuck,' complains Claire (aged 3 years) as she sits on the tractor. 'My goodness, I wonder why those wheels aren't turning,' Rosaleen the practitioner says. Jamie (aged 4 years), who was watching the wheels spinning in the mud, joins the pair. Over the next few minutes they discuss why the wheels are sticking and how to solve this problem. Claire declines Rosaleen's suggestion to get off the tractor and pull it out of the mud. Claire wants to drive out! Eventually Jamie offers an acceptable solution: 'My Granda uses long things of wood when his tractor is stuck in muck. Can we do that too?' 'What do you think Claire, will we give it a try?' Rosaleen asks. 'Ya, let's,' says Claire as she and Jamie head off to find some pieces of timber to place under the wheel. There was a problem to solve: the tractor just had to be moved. So the children together with their practitioner put on their 'thinking caps' and solved the problem. Practitioners can plan specific learning experiences to help children develop thinking and talking skills and to make use of daily opportunities to think and talk together. Some of these opportunities might arise during and after child-initiated play, in conversations at break times, when reading stories, after watching a DVD, on returning from a trip, and in small group learning experiences. The important element in promoting sustained shared thinking is encouraging children to reflect on what they experience.

Note

1. Magic here refers to events that seem to defy the laws of physical causality.

Chapter 7

Egocentrism and the preschooler

In this chapter we are going to explore a little further the concept of egocentrism in the preschooler. Piaget believed that children's thinking remains egocentric throughout the preoperational stage of cognitive development. In this chapter we will review his work and update findings on this important area of cognitive development in childhood. In particular, we will discuss the implications of egocentric thinking for children's social development. Alison Gopnik is an American psychologist and professor of psychology at the University of California, Berkeley. Let's look at an extract below, where she tells us about some of the more current work she has carried out with young children and what it tells us about their ability to take the perspective of others.

> In 1996 Betty Repacholi (now at Washington) and I found that 18-month-olds can understand that I might want one thing, whereas you want another. An experimenter showed 14- and 18-month-olds a bowl of raw broccoli and a bowl of goldfish crackers and then tasted some of each, making either a disgusted face or a happy face. Then she put her hand out and asked, 'Could you give me some?' The 18-month-olds gave her broccoli when she acted as if she liked it, even though they would not choose it for themselves. The 14-month-olds always gave her crackers. So, even at this very young age, children are not completely egocentric: they can take the perspective of another person, at least in a simple way.
>
> (Gopnik, 2010, p. 78)

This chapter will build on and extend some of the concepts introduced in chapter 6 on the preoperational world, with the particular aim of illustrating these concepts through further examples from children's real-life experiences. Young children demonstrate cognitive egocentrism when they fail to recognise that their knowledge is *not* identical to another's knowledge, that what they can see is *not* identical to what others can see. This explains, to some extent, why the very young child speaking, for example, to their parent on the phone may nod silently in answer to a question. This feature of young children's thinking has many important implications for their relationships with other people in their world. Young children may assume that their desires, wishes and emotions are identical to those of other people. More recent research on theory of mind abilities in childhood has challenged some of Piaget's assumptions about egocentrism. This research has demonstrated that during the preschool period, approximately between 3 and 6 years of age, children come to realise others may have desires different from their own and they begin to take another's perspective in trying to determine what the other person's wishes may be. The significance of these developments within the preschool period of early childhood will be discussed further with reference to the development of empathy and other pro-social behaviours.

What do we mean by egocentrism?

Egocentrism in the young child refers to a feature of *all* young children's thinking. This feature can be attributed to the fact that, at this young age, i.e. birth to 3 years of age, children do not yet have access to those cognitive resources that make it possible to step back and see things from other people's perspectives. Let's take an example to illustrate what we mean by egocentrism in the young child. During her placement experience with children 3–4 years of age, Julie, a student in early childhood education, recorded the following conversation with one of the children.

JULIE: Hi Ciara . . . did you have a nice time at the weekend? Did you do anything nice?

CIARA: Yep . . . we did lots . . . I had lots of fun playing . . . and I visited my auntie's house.

JULIE: Oh lovely. . . . And did your little brother go too?

CIARA: No . . . he's too young . . . he's just a little baby . . . my brother. Brothers are babies.

JULIE: Well, not all brothers are babies. I have a brother and he is older than me!

Ciara looks puzzled.

Ciara is seeing the world from her own perspective and as her brother is a baby, for the moment, she is assuming that all brothers are babies. Preschoolers at this age are not yet able to take that step back from themselves and tend to make the assumption that everybody thinks, feels, sees and hears the same as they do. This kind of thinking is related to not yet having the ability to *decentre*. The term decentre is one that we have come across before in chapter 3 and refers to the ability to focus on more than one aspect of an event. In terms of egocentrism in the young child, we are talking about the fact that the child is very focused or centred on their *own* thoughts and perspectives, but is not yet able to shift their focus to take on board what *other* people think and feel.

Ackermann (1996, p. 29) highlights the fact that while 4-year-old children may very well understand that someone else can have a different perspective or viewpoint to their own, what is more difficult for children to understand is that viewpoints are 'lenses, and that different lenses transform "reality" in specific ways'. To put this in simpler terms, as we will see in later sections, children as young as 3 years of age may well *understand* that other people see and think differently to them – what these young children are not yet able to do is to *interpret* or understand *exactly what* another person actually sees or thinks.

Piaget's views on egocentrism

In this section we will summarise some of the main findings that Piaget came up with based on his experiments and tasks developed to assess egocentrism in the young child. Schaffer (2006) summarises some of the key aspects of Piaget's findings on egocentrism under the headings of perceptual ego-centrism, communicative egocentrism, peer play and moral understanding in young children. Let's look at each of these in turn and reflect on how they relate to the young child in early years settings.

Perceptual egocentrism

Piaget observed that young children assume that other people see things from the same perspective as they do, even if they are facing in the opposite direction and have a different view in front of them. One of the most famous tasks that Piaget devised was known as the Three Mountain Task and is outlined below and illustrated in Figure 7.1.

Based on findings from this task, Piaget concluded that children continue to see things from their own perspective right through the preoperational period and until they are approximately 7 years of age.

Communicative egocentrism

Another form of egocentrism in childhood that Piaget drew attention to is *communicative egocentrism,* where children talk to themselves or engage in dialogue with someone else but are not conscious of the fact that the other person does not have access to the same information as they do. A very good illustration of this is the child in conversation with her father on the telephone who, when he asks if her mummy is there, replies by nodding!

Piaget himself describes communicative egocentrism when he says the child 'feels no desire to influence his hearers nor to tell them anything . . .'.

Three Mountain Task (Piaget and Inhelder 1956)

A child is seated in front of a model of three mountains of different sizes and shapes. The child is then shown photographs of the model taken from each side and asked which one corresponds to the way *they* see it – preschoolers can usually do this quite easily. A doll is then placed on the other side of the table and the child is then asked which photo corresponds to the doll's viewpoint. Most young children point to the photo corresponding to their *own* viewpoint. However, by 7 years of age, children will correctly point to the picture that represents the doll's view.

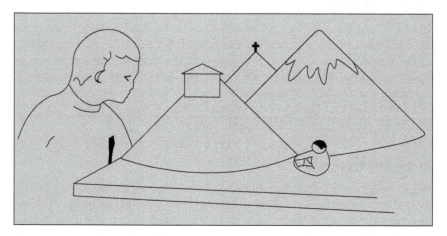

Figure 7.1. Three Mountain Task

In his observations of young children, Piaget (1962) noted that when young children were playing their communication was often non-reciprocal – in other words, they conducted a kind of a monologue in speaking to themselves, which might involve verbal repetitions of what another child was saying. Piaget saw this as an inability on the part of the child to share information with another child or adult. According to Piaget, around the age of 7 or 8, a child begins to think logically and more critically. Parallel to this development, egocentric speech disappears. However, it is worth noting that Vygotsky had a very different view of the young child's egocentric speech. Vygotsky (1986) preferred the term 'private speech' or 'self-directed speech', which for him represented a very significant cognitive function for the young child in allowing them to plan, monitor and guide themselves while they were engaged in different activities.

Egocentrism and playing with peers

Piaget also devised stages of play that coincided with his stages of cognitive development – for example, the very young child may engage in playing alone or playing alongside other children but with little interaction between them. These types of play are called solitary play and parallel play respectively. Children may find it easier to focus on their own activities and may not yet have developed the ability to link their individual contribution to those of others in order to bring about a 'co-operative product' (Schaffer, 2006, p. 131).

Egocentrism and moral understanding

As children move through the early years, they become increasingly aware of others around them and develop the ability to feel empathy – understanding of another person's feelings and sharing in those feelings (Geangu, 2009). It is believed that this ability begins to become apparent as early as in the second year of life, when more mature-like empathic concern emerges (Knafo *et al.*, 2008). Whitebread (2012) highlights that children demonstrate empathic behaviours much earlier than Piaget suggested, learning to sympathise with others and showing empathy towards other children experiencing distress or unhappiness. Most importantly, children learn empathy through their experiences and the different situations that arise for them.

However, as Piaget (1932) pointed out, during this symbolic function substage, children's understanding of morals and moral rules depends almost exclusively on the authority of their own parents. Regardless of the context and of the particular circumstances of the situation, parental rules must be adhered to at all costs. As children move through this preoperational period they become more aware of the need for mutual negotiation and the possibility of modifying and qualifying some of the rules they have learned from their parents. Later on, in interactions with their peers, children learn that rules depend on 'mutual negotiation and reciprocity' (Schaffer, 2006, p. 131).

Updating Piaget's views on egocentrism

If we stop to think about it, many of us would feel that while Piaget's Three Mountain Task is an interesting experiment and helps us think further about the ability of taking someone else's perspective, it does not enlighten us sufficiently about the very complex and differentiated abilities that emerge in early childhood with regard to egocentrism and taking another's perspective. First of all, there are many aspects to perspective taking as the ability to know what another person can *see* is quite different to knowing what another person is *thinking*.

Piaget used the term 'egocentrism' in a way that suggested that it was a unitary concept – in other words, that it developed across all aspects of development at the same time. However, more recent work has refuted this belief and suggests that the ability to take the perspective of others is domain-specific[1] – for example, the mental skills employed to understand the three domains of physical, biological and psychological phenomena have been found to develop independently and at different rates. So, as we have noted, children may be able to understand and express what someone else sees from a different perspective, but they may not yet be able to imagine how another person might think in a particular situation.

Perhaps most importantly, and as noted in chapter 6, there have been many criticisms of Piaget's tasks in assessing egocentrism in young children. Ackermann (1996) emphasises that the tasks that Piaget used to evaluate children's ability to take the perspective of others were making demands on cognitive abilities that went beyond an understanding of egocentrism. Since Piaget, researchers have used simplified tasks with materials that are more familiar and meaningful to children. One brief example of such a task is described below.

Cats on one side, dogs on the other side (Flavell, 1990)

This simple task was also devised in order to try to gain insight into the young child's ability to understand that what they can see is not always the same as what another person can see. Young children are shown a 2D piece of cardboard with the representation of a cat on one side and a dog on the other side. When presented with this task, 3- to 4-year-old children were easily able to understand that if they could see a cat, the child in front of them could see a dog.

Findings from these simplified tasks challenge Piaget's earlier findings that children remain egocentric in their thinking up to 7 years of age. These more recent findings are summarised below:

- Young children (3–4 years of age) are clearly able to understand that another person's viewpoint of a physical object may be different from their own if that object is presented from a different station point.
- Children's failure in Piaget's classical Three Mountain Task is not because they are egocentric but rather because it is very difficult for them to hold *all the possible perspectives in mind.*
- Children know very well that another person will see an object differently when they are looking at it from a different viewpoint; however, they

may not be able to *specify* what another person can see if there are many possible perspectives.

New directions in research on egocentrism and the preschooler

Piaget's work was invaluable in pointing us in the direction of so many fascinating aspects of thinking in childhood. One of these very significant features of children's thinking is egocentrism, as we have been seeing in previous sections. We now know, however, that Piaget underestimated the ability of the young child to take the perspective of others. Nevertheless, his work identified a central challenge in social-cognitive activity: the challenge of separating one's own viewpoint from that of other people's (Miller, 2010). Since Piaget, however, there has been a wealth of research and work carried out to further explore the extent to which children can take the perspective of others and how these abilities influence and impact on their social understanding and behaviours. We will review some of this work, first of all, under the broad heading of social cognition and then, more specifically, under the heading of theory of mind abilities in children.

Social cognition and perspective taking in preschoolers

Social cognition is at the heart of children's ability to get along with other people and to see things from their point of view. Miller (2010) suggests that the development of social-cognitive understanding is one of the most important achievements of childhood cognitive development. As we have seen, children gradually become less egocentric, learning that other people's perspectives differ from their own, which helps them to communicate more effectively. Preschool children also develop their ability to understand how other people think and feel, which allows them to reflect on other people's desires, motives and intentions. One of the most natural and at the same time invaluable activities that children engage in – play – contributes significantly to promoting and supporting these abilities in children.

Brennan (2012) emphasises the importance of play for children's understanding of rules and social conventions. As highlighted by Vygotsky, children learn to regulate their behaviours and emotions and play activities support them in learning to coordinate and align their behaviours and emotions with those of other children and, more broadly, other adults around them. In this process, they internalise rules as a natural way of thinking and learn to think in a shared way. The development of social cognition is an excellent example of how cognitive and social development is interdependent with one aspect of this development constantly influencing other aspects of development.

Self and other: the origins of empathy

Empathy can be defined as the ability to perceive or imagine the emotional state or condition of another person, and thereby come to experience a similar affective state (Eisenberg *et al.*, 1991; de Waal, 2008; Geangu, 2009). Practitioners working with children in the early years place much emphasis on helping children learn to be aware of and respond to the feelings of other children in their environment. Underpinning the ability to effectively respond to the feelings of others is the ability to clearly distinguish between the needs of the child themselves and the needs of others around them. So, the development of empathy in the early years is associated with:

*   clearly understanding that you are a separate entity to those around you; and
*   being able to take the perspective of those around you.

Without these abilities, children showing distress at others' distress may simply be a passive expression of discomfort and may not lead to more active manifestations of empathic behaviour (Van der Mark *et al.*, 2002). Contesting Piaget's view that children remain egocentric in their thinking throughout the preschool age, a body of more recent research indicates that the beginnings of empathic behaviours can be traced to the second half of the first year in a baby's life (Knafo *et al.*, 2008).

In a recent study of helping and cooperation in 14-month-olds, Warneken and Tomasello (2007) found that at 14 months the child could *understand* the unfulfilled goal of another (reaching for something but not being able to attain) and was also able to *help* the other person to achieve their goal by reaching for the object and passing it on to the adult. However it was not until 18 months that children showed more a developed ability to help and *cooperate* with others. The authors make some interesting comments on how the cognitive demands of helping and cooperating are quite distinct with regard to their intentional structure (Warneken & Tomasello, 2007). For example, helping might be easier for children as the child needs to understand what another individual intends to do – in other words, the child needs to know what actions the other person carried out or wanted to carry out in order to achieve his or her individual goal. Cooperation, on the other hand, requires the ability to form a shared goal and to combine or coordinate plans of action toward that goal.

What is most interesting for us to focus on in terms of these findings is the fact that, in contrast to Piaget's findings on egocentrism in childhood thinking, we have evidence of the ability to take another's perspective in children just two months into their second year.

Egocentrism and theory of mind

Piaget's contribution to our understanding of egocentrism in children's thinking has been challenged and updated, as we can see. Theory of mind refers to the ability to understand mental states as, for example, beliefs, desires, intentions, in ourselves and in other people (Miller, 2011). Much of the research carried out under this umbrella term focused on children in the early years. A more positive and comprehensive picture of preschoolers' abilities than Piaget's has been generated by this more recent work. Piaget has been criticised for contributing to a 'deficit' view of the child – focusing more on what the child cannot do than on the many competencies that children have. To some extent we might agree with this view. However, Piaget set the scene for so much of the insightful research that followed in the latter part of the 20th century and up to the present time. Theory of mind research has provided an invaluable corrective to the earlier literature on social cognition, which had characterised the preschool period primarily in negative terms.

Below is a brief summary of some of the key findings that have emerged from this body of work:

*   By the age of 2, children can quite easily tell the difference between things in the mind and things in the external world (Kavanaugh, 2006). A good illustration of this is the 2-year-old's ability to distinguish in pretend play between an object – a chair – and thoughts about the object – the chair as a car.
*   Children also show a basic understanding of there being a difference between what they want and what another person wants (Meltzoff *et al.*, 1999).
*   The language used by the 2-year-old also reflects this developing awareness as children talk about what they and others want and like and feel, and when they are 3 they talk about what other people think and know (Bartsch & Wellman, 1995).
*   One of the most significant findings from the work carried out by theory of mind researchers is that there is a very significant development in children's thinking around the age of 4. At this age children begin to become aware that the thoughts that they have in their minds may not be true in reality. This was illustrated in a very well-known experiment called the False Belief Task, outlined below.

False Belief Task (Perner et al., 1987)

This task involves working with 3- and 4-year-old children and comparing their responses on the task. The researcher shows a box of Smarties to the child and asks the child what they think is in the box before they open it. Naturally, the child typically replies 'Smarties'. Then the researcher opens the box and shows the child that in fact there are pencils in the box, not Smarties as they had believed. The child is usually surprised by this revelation (and often disappointed at the absence of sweeties in the box). The researcher then says to the child 'we are now going to put the pencils back in the box and close the box. I am going to ask Jake to come in to the room. What do you think he will say when I ask what is in the box?'

Findings from this experiment indicate that 3-year-old children usually assume that their friend or the next child will know that the box has pencils inside. It has been suggested this is because they are not differentiating between what they are thinking and what another person is thinking. By contrast, 4-year-old children will always respond by saying that the next person will also assume that there are Smarties (not pencils) in the box.

When we think a little about what these abilities might mean for the child's behaviour, we realise that between 3 and 4 years of age there is an important watershed or transition in children's ability to represent what other people think and believe. The 4-year-old child has developed the ability to take that step back from another person's mind and to understand that what they are thinking is not the same as what the other person may be thinking. This allows the 4-year-old to enter a more complex world where they have greater access to the beliefs and intentions of others. This new ability to read and understand better what others might be thinking, of course, allows the preschooler access to new behaviours such as manipulation and playing mind games on those others they are engaging with!

So far we have focused on the social skills that are associated with the growing ability to become less egocentric through developing an ability to take the perspective of other people. Most importantly this involves learning to understand that other people's beliefs, feelings and intentions are quite distinct from our own. In the following chapter, when we explore the second substage of Piaget's preoperational stage, we will see how egocentrism may limit the young child's performance on skills related to number and scientific concepts.

Implications for practice

As Piaget's findings on egocentrism and the child of preschool age are very different from what we now know about children of this age, the implications for practice outlined below do not draw on Piaget's theory to any great extent but rather draw on some of the more recent findings that have emerged from research into children's minds and their abilities to take the perspectives of others in post-Piagetian research.

- Social cognitive abilities can be supported and promoted within early years settings. Much work has been carried out on helping children understand the consequences of their actions and in helping children to successfully resolve conflicts and disputes with other children. Early years practitioners can promote and encourage children to think about their own and other children's emotions by encouraging them to verbalise feelings and by asking individual children to explain or talk about their feelings from their own perspective. Suggestions offered by the child for resolving conflict can be restated by the early years practitioner and discussed with the other child or children (Whitebread, 2012). In this way, children are encouraged to negotiate and to share their feelings and responses with others. Interventions that focus on helping children become aware of negative social-cognitive patterns can help children to alter those beliefs in a positive direction, which in turn can have a beneficial impact on their social behaviour and social acceptance (Miller, 2010).
- Relationships are at the very heart of early learning and development (NCCA, 2009). As we have seen, the very young child engages with others and develops an awareness of other people and their needs through these interactions. While many of these interactions may happen naturally, early years professionals can create and provide useful opportunities for these interactions to be developed. Strategies to help practitioners and adults work with children in more effective ways in order to promote the child's understanding of themselves and people around them are outlined in *Aistear: the Early Childhood Curriculum Framework* in Ireland (NCCA, 2009). Building on children's dispositions, knowledge, understandings, skills, attitudes and values, the adult follows the children's leads and collaborates with the children in exploring together different ways of thinking about things, looking at different perspectives, while all the time trying to connect with what children already know and understand.
- The possibilities for encouraging shared attention in children as young as 1 or 2 years of age are supported by more recent research in the early years. Smidt (2011) refers to the potential of bridging the gap between shared *attention* and shared *intention* in young children through a heightened focus on joint action. Specifically, creating possibilities for young children to interact with others, to share the focus of attention in their activities, can encourage and promote awareness of different perspectives on a shared task. One aspect of shared attention that is highlighted by Smidt (2009) is what she terms *targeted feedback*. In other words, by reflecting back to children our views on what they do and how they respond to our requests, we can heighten their awareness

of how their perspectives may differ from other people's in their lives. Early childhood professionals can play a significant role in generating opportunities for shared interactions with children and in providing targeted feedback to children as part of these interactions.

• Children's abilities to take the perspectives of others can be supported and promoted through play, perhaps especially in socio-dramatic play activities. The potential for exploring how it feels to be somebody else is great when children become involved in role play activities with other children. As Hughes (2003) emphasises, the child can play at being mother, father, teacher, police officer and can even experiment with playing more than one role at a time.

Note

1. Different mental mechanisms exist for different cognitive domains.

Chapter 8

The preoperational world
Intuitive thought substage

In this chapter we will focus on the second substage of Piaget's preoperational stage of cognitive development, the intuitive thought substage – spanning the age of 4–7 years. Piaget used the word *intuitive* in the second substage to capture children's intuitive knowledge and curiosity about the world around them. However, according to Piaget, this knowledge still often lacked the ability to reason and rationalise the principles underlying this knowledge.

Four key aspects of cognitive development are highlighted in this second substage of the preoperational world and we will look at these in some detail below.

Pursuit of logical reasoning: the child begins to ask questions and look for logical explanations for what happens in the world around them.
Classification: the preoperational child shows knowledge about different *kinds of things* and categories of objects, but there are still some limitations to the extent to which they can cross-classify.
Seriation: preoperational children still find it difficult to arrange things in order – i.e. to put things in order from the biggest to the smallest in size.
Conservation: preoperational children show some difficulty in understanding that although something may change in appearance, the essence or the original property is conserved, or stays the same.

Pursuit of logical reasoning: how things work and why things take place

Causal knowledge is arguably the most significant knowledge we can have, uniting our apparently disparate experiences, allowing us to make new predictions about the events we have yet to experience, and most significantly, allowing us to imagine new possibilities and intervene in the world to reshape it in significant ways. We could argue, in fact, that causal knowledge underlies our distinctively human ability to control and construct our environment.

(Gopnik, 2012, p. 628)

Children have an intuition about how and why things happen and intuitively tend to understand certain phenomena, but they have not yet put all the pieces together and this is what they are seeking in their endless questioning and pursuit of logical reasoning.

Darragh is 4 years old. It is his second year at ABC Montessori. He loves construction. He plays with small wooden blocks indoors, and large planks and blocks outdoors. He plays with Lego and he loves to create large and small constructions with junk materials. On this occasion, Darragh was busy with junk craft when I arrived. He was totally engrossed in it and was oblivious to everyone around him, so I sat down close to him and started to video tape him. At first he paid no attention to me or to anyone else until a girl came over and started to ask him about his construction. As time went on, he enlisted the help of Pat with the sticking tape. He seemed happy to talk about his work and I asked him some questions about it to help me understand. He told me that he had made two dens, one for the good guys and one for the baddies. The bad guys were tightly taped into a small box that was then enveloped in wrapping paper 'so that the baddies can't get out', but the good guys were housed in a chocolates tray which was taped to a milk carton 'so that they can jump out'. Darragh considered this to be a really good plan and made it clear that he was proud of his construction and had invested a lot of thought in the work.

(Brennan, 2004)

As we have seen throughout this book, children have a desire to understand and make sense of the world, to develop and test hypotheses and to arrive at logical conclusions. We can see this evidenced in Darragh's clear explanations of why he has developed two different types of dens. Piaget underestimated the extent to which children can engage in logical reasoning and we will explore that further later in this chapter. However, he drew attention to the growing curiosity and 'intuitive' knowledge that children accumulate in this stage of their development.

Children begin to ask questions around the age of 3 and during the following years they are relentless in their pursuit of answers to questions about everything under and including the sun! *Why does the sun shine? Where does the sun go at night?* The preoperational child's vocal curiosity is a reflection of their growing ability and interest in reasoning and thinking logically about the world around them. Attentive to the detail of what is happening in the world around them, they now want to explore the mechanisms underlying these events, mechanisms that go some way to explaining them. Piaget used detailed interviews and observations to gain insight into some of the features of reasoning in early childhood.

Entering the child's mind

Piaget's 'clinical interview' involved asking children a series of open-ended questions. Piaget modelled the format of asking these questions on clinical practice in order to 'diagnose' the type of thinking the child was using (Labinowicz, 1985). For instance, he asked children, 'What makes clouds move?'

> In Piaget's clinical interview method, the adult interviewer involves the child in conversations through verbally-presented problems in the context of physical materials. In order to achieve its goal of exploring children's reasoning on intellectual tasks, the method seeks to encourage each child to verbalise freely and to interact with the objects, thus providing a basis for the interviewer's hypotheses about the underlying thinking. These hypotheses about the child's perspective of the problem are tested by spontaneously invented questions based on earlier responses. The interviewer's role is to encourage the child to consider further, think more specifically or rethink the process used in arriving at a solution.
>
> (Labinowicz, 1985, p. 26)

Based on analysis of the changing features within children's answers as they moved through early childhood, Piaget identified the following patterns of ability to reason according to the child's age (DeHart *et al.*, 2004).

Level 1: It is what it seems

Younger children rely on the appearances of an event in order to explain the world. They are still somewhat egocentric in their perceptions – they may feel that clouds move because the children themselves are moving; the sun goes down because the children themselves go to sleep. Of course, children's reasoning at this age makes a lot of sense. Think sometimes of how you might be sitting in a train that is not moving. If the train at the next track starts to move, for a moment you may be tricked into thinking that you are moving. These kinds of experiences influence children's explanations of things happening in the world around them.

ADULT: What makes clouds move?
CHILD: When we move along they move along also.
ADULT: Can you make them move?
CHILD: Yes.
ADULT: But you tell me that they move when somebody walks.
CHILD: They always move. The cats, when they walk, and then the dogs, they make the clouds move.
(Piaget, 1930/1969, p. 62. Cited in DeHart *et al.*, 2004)

Level 2: Belief in the all-powerful

In this second level of reasoning, Piaget suggested that children attribute causes to certain events using the concept of an all-powerful force that controls objects and events. For example, they may attribute the cause of an event to God:

ADULT: What makes the clouds move along?
CHILD: God does.
ADULT: How?
CHILD: He pushes them.
>   (Piaget, 1930/1969, p. 63. Cited in DeHart *et al.*, 2004)

Level 3: Improbable causes

As children move through early childhood they start to explain events around them in a way that resembles adult reasoning. One of the ways in which this happens is when children begin using causes in nature to explain natural phenomena in the world around them. An example of this might be the rays of sun pushing clouds along. While such causes are understandable and reasonable to some extent, as we can see, these causes may still be rather improbable.

ADULT: What makes the clouds move along?
CHILD: It's the sun.
ADULT: How?
CHILD: With its rays. It pushes the clouds.
>   (Piaget, 1930/1969, p. 65. Cited in DeHart *et al.*, 2004)

Level 4: Plausible but incomplete

Piaget believed that children at this stage begin to approach an adult explanation, even though their explanation is still quite incomplete. So while elements of truth are present and provide some basis for explanation of events, there are missing details that children are unable to provide at this early age.

ADULT: What makes the clouds move along?
CHILD: Because they have a current.
ADULT: What is this current?
CHILD: It's in the clouds.
>   (Piaget, 1930/1969, p. 72. Cited in DeHart *et al.*, 2004)

Piaget suggested that children do not become capable of mature reasoning about causation until well into middle childhood, but other researchers have shown that the level of preschoolers' causal reasoning is influenced by the familiarity and complexity of the problems posed. As has been pointed out by many authors, some of the problems that Piaget was posing to these young children were complex and demanded a very sophisticated level of under-standing of the physical world. However, more recent work with young children has demonstrated that in situations that are personal and meaningful to children, these young children are capable of providing complete and rea-sonable explanations for events in the world around them (Wellman & Gelman, 1998). For example, a 5-year-old child may well be able to give a logical explanation for why the wheels of her bicycle turn and what makes them turn.

In the intuitive thought substage, children begin to question and explore concepts of time and chronology and this is nicely illustrated in the conversation between Georgia (3 years, 7 months) and her Mum about Steph (Georgia's friend), outlined below by Arnold (1999):

GEORGIA: Steph is three or four?

MUM: Three, nearly four. I think she'll be four in October or November.

GEORGIA: When me going to be four?

MUM: January the 26th.

GEORGIA: Me going to be four first?

MUM: No, you're not.

GEORGIA: Why is Steph going to be four first?

MUM: Because she was in her mummy's tummy before you were in mine.

GEORGIA: Why?

MUM: Because her mummy was pregnant before me.

Georgia is not satisfied with simple answers but wants to probe further. She is using language and questions to expand her schemas and accommodate information acquired from her present experiences to adapt knowledge based on past experiences. The process of equilibration continues but in the intuitive thought substage, language is an important tool that allows the child to identify and seek the missing pieces in their knowledge and understanding of the world around them.

Magical thinking: developing awareness of the boundaries between fantasy and reality

In his interviews with children in the preoperational stage of cognitive devel-opment, Piaget (1929) observed that their thinking sometimes reflected con-fusion between thoughts that occurred in their minds and resultant events in the external world. For Piaget these 'errors' in children's thinking patterns gave rise to a variety of mistaken beliefs about the causal relations between the mind and the physical world. Piaget also suggested that children continue to rely on magical explanations to explain events in the world until they are at least 7 or 8 years of age. However, more recent research suggests that by 3 years of age children have considerable knowledge about the boundaries between fantasy and reality and that it is typically between the ages of 18 months and 3 years that children engage in magical thinking in terms of explaining physical causality. More recently, Rosengren and Hickling (2000) refute some of Piaget's findings on magical thinking and argue that developmental progression in this thinking is not uniform or universal. The process is strongly influenced by the characteristics of the child, significant older individuals and the wider culture. Children's explanations for events in the physical world shift with the context in which the individual child is developing.

One of the reasons that preschoolers may tend to provide imaginary and sometimes far-fetched explanations is that, as yet, they have not grasped what a good explanation for something is. For this reason, when they do not have the knowledge to explain something, they may rely on their imagination to invent what they might consider a plausible explanation. With experience and growing knowledge of specific causes and effects, they develop a foundation for a more mature and abstract concept of causation (DeHart *et al.*, 2004).

Classification

A typical daily task for the young child in crèche or preschool is to tidy up games and toys and to put things away where they belong. Most young children develop familiarity with the categories of objects they have been playing with and are usually able to put these objects back into the area in which similar objects are contained. This is classification in a very basic form. Piaget suggested that children do not learn a complete understanding of classification until they are in the concrete operational stage of cognitive development. Shortly, we will look at how Piaget came to these conclusions. We will see that many young children have the ability to classify objects, but may not always be familiar with the names of colours, shapes, materials, and this may be mistaken for lack of knowledge or ability to classify. This problem can be overcome by phrasing questions in a particular way as we will see in the extract below from Kirova and Bhargava (2002, np):

> To help Rachel develop the ability to classify by function or association, during clean-up time Laura asked her, 'Can you put the things that you draw with together in this box, please?' or 'Can you find in the play centre all the things a doctor uses and put them in one place, please?' During dramatic play, Laura asked the children to gather everything necessary to set up a grocery store so that Goldilocks could buy more groceries to make porridge for the bears.

While preschool children may not yet have a clear understanding of class inclusion and exclusion, if we use specific questions and when these tasks are related to personal experiences, these young children very often demonstrate partial understanding of the concept (Kirova & Bhargava, 2002). With developing language abilities, the child will move on to be able to classify using two or more attributes.

We have talked in previous chapters about how children use schemas to organise their thoughts and ideas around events and objects. And we have talked about how children's schemas become more complex over time to include categories and sub-categories of objects, animals, plants and even people. The preoperational child has developed complex schemas to organise their thinking, but according to Piaget they still have some difficulties with identifying and sorting together different kinds of things (Smith *et al.*, 2003).

Piagetian task on classification skills

One of the most well-known tasks that Piaget devised for assessing children's classification skills was as follows:

> Children are given a box containing 18 brown beads and 2 white beads. All the beads are wooden. The researcher asks 'Are there more brown beads than wooden beads?' Typically the preoperational child will answer 'brown beads'.

According to Piaget, this difficulty arises because the child seems to find it hard to consider the class of 'all beads' at the same time as considering the subset of 'brown beads'. There are other possible reasons that help us understand why children do not succeed on this task. The question 'Are there more brown beads or more wooden beads?' is a complex question that requires the child to hold in memory a number of representations. Piaget has been criticised for the nature of his tasks and the complex and sometimes strange wording used to explore these concepts in young children. Beads are perhaps neither a familiar nor meaningful kind of object to the child. Could this contribute to why the child might find the question difficult to answer correctly?

More recent work by McGarrigle and Donaldson (1974) used the example of toy cows – three black and one white – lying asleep on their sides. When the children were asked 'Are there more black cows or more cows?' they tended to answer incorrectly. Could this have been because they thought it was a silly question?! However, when they were asked 'Are there more black cows or more *sleeping* cows?', preoperational children were more likely to answer correctly. If we think about it, what the children are demonstrating in these experiments seems to be a difficulty attending to more than one feature at a time. A concept that has recurred repeatedly in Piaget's theory, centration, seems to be very important in explaining children's incorrect answers on these tasks.

Piaget also explored preoperational children's emerging understanding of classifying and categorising objects and focused on the difficulty they have in sorting objects according to two or more properties. Piaget gave children different coloured shapes and asked them to sort those that went together into different groups (Inhelder & Piaget, 1964). In the simplest form of this task there were only two colours (e.g. red and blue) and two shapes (circles and squares). Piaget found that:

- Youngest preschoolers would sometimes sort correctly according to one dimension – either shape or colour. For example, they might put all the red circles and squares in one pile and all the blue ones in another.
- So grouping all the red blocks and all the blue blocks together is no problem. Grouping the blocks into circles or squares would also be possible for the older preoperational child.
- However, when asked to group together all the *red circular blocks* and all the *blue square blocks* – the challenge is typically too great. Older preschoolers were more consistent in their sorting until by age 5 they were quite good at classifying along one dimension. Even the 5-year-olds, however, still focused on only a single characteristic (e.g. colour).
- Ten-year-olds, in contrast, would sort using both dimensions simultaneously – putting all the blue squares in one pile, all the blue circles in another, all the red squares in a third and the red circles in a fourth.

What have we learned about children's classification abilities since Piaget?

Studies that have used more child-friendly approaches and provided more guidance to children have found that children can sort consistently along one dimension at an earlier age. However, in general, preoperational children still showed some of the limitations that Piaget had highlighted. DeHart *et al.* (2004) draw attention to a series of studies carried out by Philip Zelazo and his colleagues outlined below.

Things that make a noise and things that don't make a noise
(Zelazo et al., 1995)

Children are given rules for sorting pictures into two boxes. The rules are as follows:

Fish go into one box and birds go into another box.

Things that make noise go into one box and things that don't make noise go into another box.

1. Two and a half-year-olds can generally tell which box a picture belongs in if asked 'Is this a bird? Is this a fish?', but cannot sort even when guided by adults.
2. Three-year-olds can follow sorting rules consistently, but may have difficulty if the category changes (e.g. from sorting by colour to sorting by shape).
3. Four-year-olds can follow rules consistently and can switch to a new category without difficulty.

So, as we have seen so many times in previous chapters, Piaget seems to have underestimated the age at which children understand the concept of category – very young children (e.g. as young as 2½ years) seem to know the difference between different classes of things but may find the added instruction to put things in separate boxes more challenging. Gopnik *et al.* (2001) have also explored the young child's ability to classify and conclude that even at 2 years of age, children are like scientists classifying and reclassifying objects. Krogh and Slentz (2001) draw attention to the fact that children learn about different kinds of things through their everyday activities, as they outline below:

> When helping her mum to put away the groceries, 3-year-old Lauren is learning through the experience of putting some groceries in the refrigerator and others on the shelf that things that feel cold should go one place while warmer objects go to the other. Without having a sophisticated understanding of abstract principles such as temperature and keeping food fresh through freezing, Lauren intuitively builds knowledge of knowing where certain kinds of things should be stored. In the same way, children in early years settings can be provided with a wealth of opportunities through which they can develop their classification skills. The essential element is that the materials and activities relate to the developmental levels of the children, and that there are specific learning objectives.

Seriation: putting things in order

Closely related to the ability to classify and categorise the world about us is the ability to identify a sequence or order to a series of objects. Going from first to last may involve increased height, darkening shades of a single colour, increased width, and so on (Krogh and Slentz, 2001). Piaget used the term 'seriation' to describe this ability and developed a task requiring children

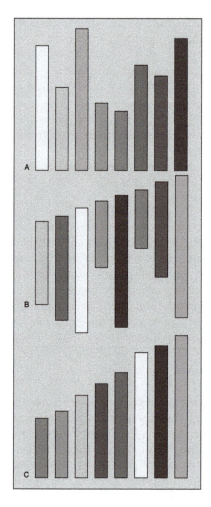

Figure 8.1. Seriation task

to arrange sticks of different lengths into order from the smallest to the largest.

For example, if you were to place 10 straws of different lengths on a table (A, above) and ask children to order them according to their length, preoperational children may group the straws into three or four bundles of 'short' or 'tall' straws rather than come up with the correct ordering of straws shown in example C, from the shortest to the tallest. Interestingly, these younger children have been found to attempt to order a series of objects by lining up the tops of the sticks but, at the same time, tend to ignore the bottom of the objects (example B). Putting objects in a sequence according to size is challenging for children as they are still focusing on one aspect at a time. This kind of task emphasises a quantitative dimension to knowledge and we will spend some time looking into the young child's increasing grasp of numbers and quantity later in this chapter and also in chapter 9.

The following extract from an article by Kirova and Bhargava (2002, np) illustrates the importance of preschoolers' play activities in helping us understand their growing knowledge and abilities related to the concept of numbers, classification and conservation.

Laura has just finished reading the story *Goldilocks and the Three Bears* to her preschool class. She announces that it is now time for free play. Four-year-old Rachel looks around the room for a while and walks over to the dramatic play/housekeeping centre. Today this centre is equipped with dolls, other soft toys, cups, plates, plastic silverware, plastic food items, a table, chairs and some dress-up clothes. Rachel picks up an oversized shirt and slips her feet into 'mummy shoes'. She then brings out three stuffed bears of different sizes from the collection and places them around the table. As she seats the bears on three chairs, she mutters under her breath, 'You are Papa Bear' (picking the largest bear), 'you are the Mummy Bear' (picking the medium-sized bear), 'and you are Baby Bear' (picking the smallest bear). Rachel then walks to the shelf and pulls out one plate and places it before Papa Bear; she walks back to the shelf to get a second plate and places it before Mama Bear; and then she makes one last trip to pick up a plate to place before Baby Bear. Next Rachel walks to the shelf and picks up a collection of spoons of different sizes. She is now joined by 5-year-old Tiffany, who tells her that the biggest bear needs the biggest spoon, the medium bear the medium spoon, and baby bear the smallest spoon. 'Remember, like the bears' story Ms. Laura read us.' Rachel looks at Tiffany and then at the spoons, then randomly places a spoon before each bear. Tiffany immediately takes over and rearranges the spoons according to the size of the bears. Rachel watches for a few seconds and then walks away.

In the observation above, Rachel demonstrated her knowledge of the mathematical concept of classification by choosing *only* the bears from a larger collection of dolls and toys. Moreover, when Rachel decides on which bear is the biggest in order to allocate this bear to the role of Papa, she demonstrates her knowledge of seriation – the ability to order the bears in size from biggest to smallest. More sophisticated knowledge of seriation is evidenced by Tiffany when she rearranges the spoons to correspond with the size of the bears after Rachel had placed the spoons randomly. More importantly, however, Tiffany demonstrated her ability to verbalise what needed to be done so that each bear received the appropriate size of spoon.

As we can see from this observation of children's play above, children learn through meaningful, naturalistic, active learning experiences (Kirova & Bhargava, 2002). As these authors highlight, early years professionals can play a central role in generating opportunities to develop materials and interactions that can help young children develop and expand their understanding of mathematics in a meaningful way.

Conservation: it's not what it seems

As adults we may tend to take for granted some of the very complex abilities we have in terms of how we reason about quantity and the concept of number. We know how to count and subtract and how to measure quantities in different ways. Most relevant to the area of conservation is the ability to understand what kind of transformations change the amount of a substance (DeHart *et al.*, 2004). For example, as adults we clearly understand that if we pour our coffee from a small paper cup into a large mug, although the quantity may *appear* to be less, in essence the quantity remains the same. However, if we add milk or hot water to the mug of coffee, the quantity changes or increases. Similarly, if we empty out some of the coffee from the mug, the quantity changes and decreases. Other examples of these transformations might be breaking a biscuit in half so that there are now two separate pieces. The young preoperational child might assume that because there are two pieces, there is more biscuit or the quantity has increased. The older child, in Piaget's concrete operational period, clearly understands that two halves of one biscuit is equal to one whole biscuit – the appearance has changed but the quantity remains the same.

So, the key knowledge that is central to the child's understanding of the concept of conservation includes understanding what kinds of transformations *change* the amount of a substance and what kinds do not (DeHart *et al.*, 2004). Let's consider a variation on one of Piaget's tasks of conservation.

Conservation of mass

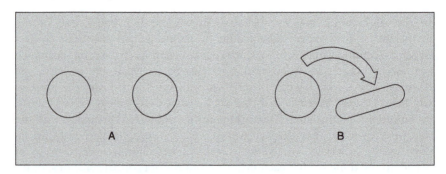

Figure 8.2. Conservation of mass task

> Two playdough balls of equal size are shown to Max (4 years of age).
> Max is asked the question 'Are they the same size or does one have
> more playdough in it than the other?' Max answers that they are the
> same. Then, while Max looks on, the researcher takes one ball of
> playdough and rolls it lengthwise into a shape resembling a sausage
> (Figure 8.2). The researcher then asks Max the same question again
> 'Are they the same size or does one have more playdough in it than the
> other?' Max replies (pointing to the sausage-shaped playdough) 'This
> one has more'.

It is interesting that although Max has watched the transformation take place
and has witnessed the fact that no material has been added or taken away
from the original ball of playdough, he is not able to *conserve* substance – in
other words, Max does not think of the amount of playdough as the same
while its length and width are changing. Phillips (1969) points out that
(i) since nothing has been added or removed, the sausage could be made
back into the original ball and (ii) every change in height is compensated
for by a change in breadth, leaving the total quantity what it was in the
beginning.

Three features of children's thought have been highlighted as contributing
to a lack of understanding of the concept of conservation. Let's spend a
moment considering these features.

Reversibility

Reversible means 'capable of being returned to its point of origin' (Phillips,
1969, p. 60). If we apply this principle to mathematical concepts, we can say
that every mathematical or logical operation is reversible. For example:

> If there are 5 children at circle time and Katie joins them, then there are
> 6 children at circle time. If Katie has to leave circle time, then there are
> 5 people at circle time again.

Understanding these simple and obvious transformations and reversible
operations is central to being able to grasp the concept of conservation.

Centration

Centration, or centering, is a term we have come across many times. This
refers to a child's tendency to focus attention on just one aspect or detail of a
particular event. As a result of this exclusive focus on one single aspect of an
event, the child is unable to process information from other aspects or details

of the event. For example, when answering the above question about the ball or sausage of playdough, the child is focusing exclusively on one aspect of these appearances – the length of the sausage, as opposed to the length and the diameter of the ball of playdough.

States versus transformations

Children in the preoperational stage of cognitive development have a tendency to focus on the end state or outcome of an action rather than on the means to this end state (DeHart *et al.*, 2004). In fact Max is most likely focusing on the successive *states* of the display (i.e. playdough looks more when flattened to be shaped into a sausage) rather than the transformations by which one state is changed into another. As Phillips (1969, p. 64) points out, 'it is as though the child were viewing a series of still pictures instead of the movie that the adult sees . . . they are unable to integrate a series of states or conditions into a coherent whole – namely, a *transformation*'.

So, conservation is the idea that the amount of something remains the same, or is conserved, despite changes in its form, shape or appearance. In the following sections we consider the different types of conservation concepts that Piaget's theory drew attention to and the associated tasks that Piaget used to assess these abilities in young children.

Conservation of liquid

In the conservation of liquid task outlined below, older children in the concrete operations stage are able to *conserve* – specifically, they are able to conserve or hold on to the original amount or quantity of water despite the change in appearance. So, perhaps younger children are attending to one aspect – height or width – and not focusing on other very relevant information. Think back to our young sensorimotor babies gradually incorporating more and more details about events – and we can see that this gradual expansion of knowledge is continuing in these preoperational years.

Tall, skinny glass of water vs short, fat glass of water

A preoperational child sits at a table where an adult pours water from one shaped glass to another. The adult invites the child to watch as she pours water from a short, fat glass into a tall, skinny glass. No water is taken away. No water is added.

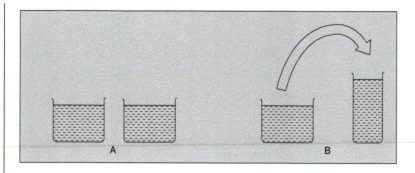

Figure 8.3. Conservation of liquid task

The adult asks the child 'Do you think there is more water in the glass now? Do you think there is less water in the glass now? Or do you think there is the same amount of water in the glass now?' Typically, the young child will tend to say that there is more water in the tall, skinny glass because he or she is focusing on one aspect of the process – the height of the glass. However, Piaget found that children in the concrete operations stage are able to understand that there is the same amount of water in the glass, despite the change of appearance.

Conservation of number

A child is shown two rows of seven coins and these coins are arranged so that the rows of coins are the same length. The child and experimenter discuss the rows of coins and once the child agrees that each row has the same number of coins, the experimenter spreads out the coins in one of the rows so that one row is longer than the other, although the number of coins in each row remains the same. The experimenter now asks if one row has more or if they both have the same number of coins. Preschoolers typically respond that the longer row has more coins.

These younger children do not yet seem to be able to grasp that superficial changes in the appearance of a quantity do not mean that there has been any fundamental change in that quantity. For example, if you have five dolls standing in a line, and then you can arrange them so that they are standing in a circle, this does not mean that there has been any alteration in the number of dolls. If nothing is added or subtracted from a quantity, then it remains the same (i.e. it is conserved). Grasping that the dolls in the

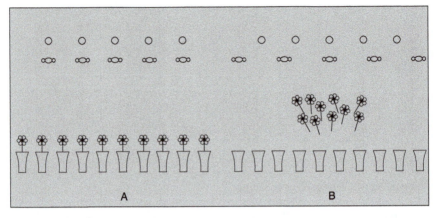

Figure 8.4. Conservation of number task

circle are the same in number as the dolls in a line is an example of conservation of number.

Returning more specifically to some of the tasks we have outlined above when assessing children's ability to conserve, it is interesting to reflect on the particular challenges that these young children face when they are engaging in these tasks. DeHart *et al.* (2004) suggest that the children are overwhelmed by the appearance of the longer row and ignore the fact that no coins have been added to it or taken away from the shorter row. Think back to what we said earlier in this chapter about young children's inability to decentre, which results in their focusing on only one aspect of an event or action (in this case, the length of the row). It is possible to also suggest that young children are likely to be influenced by the fact that the adult has changed something in the arrangement and then proceeds to ask a question about whether there is a difference between the two rows. Given children's difficulty to decentre and process more than one aspect of the event, it is possible that they are not thinking in terms of numbers but rather presume that there must be a difference.

Some more recent research in the area of children's ability to conserve number is illustrated in work by Rochel Gelman. Gelman (1972) showed children two plates, one containing a row of two toy mice, the other a row of three. The task was framed as a game where the children were told they were going to play a game in which they had to identify the 'winning' plate. At the beginning of the task, the researcher pointed to the plate with three mice and said it would always be the winning plate. The children were then asked to uncover a plate and decide if it was the winner. Whenever a child identified the plate with three mice as the winner, they were rewarded with a small prize. After some time, the researcher changed the plate with three mice, either removing a mouse or moving the mice closer together or farther apart. Even 3- and 4-year-olds continued to define the winning plate by number of mice, not row length. Interestingly, many children failed to notice such a change but almost all the children noticed *removal* of a mouse. A more recent variation on this task involves setting out two rows of chocolates for young children of 3 and 4 years of age. Instead of asking the children which row has more chocolates, the experimenter asked the children which row of chocolates they would prefer to eat. Findings showed that children as young as 2 chose to eat the row with most chocolates, no matter how they were spaced (Blakemore and Frith, 2005).

DeHart *et al.* (2004) draw attention to the fact that all the children use a rule of some kind to determine their answers in Gelman's conservation of numbers task. All of the children also showed some understanding that addition to a set *increases* its number and subtraction *decreases* its number. The rules used by children of different ages varied in sophistication and effectiveness, according to their ages. Three types of rules were identified as follows:

Primitive rules (2- and 3-year-olds): These youngest children ignored the initial number of items in each group and always said a group *added to* now had *more* than the other group and a group *subtracted from* always had less than another group.

Qualitative rules (4- and 5-year-olds): Most 4- and 5-year-olds used a rule that took into account any initial difference between the two groups, but did not consider the magnitude of the difference. These rules centred around the terms: *less than, equal to, more than*. When the initial groups differed by more than one, this rule led to inevitable errors. For example, if the groups initially had five and seven, and one more was added to the smaller group, a child using this rule would mistakenly say the two groups had become equal.

Quantitative rules (6- to 7-year-olds): Most of these older children had developed a rule that took into account the magnitude of any difference between the initial groups – that is, the quantities involved. This enabled them to give consistently correct answers.

The use of three rules is related to the development of conservation of number. Children who use the primitive rule do not show any grasp of number conservation, while many of those who use the qualitative rule appear to be somewhere in-between. Those who use the quantitative rule tend to achieve number conservation. This finding lends support to Piaget's belief that children's understanding of number conservation is related to their general understanding of numbers. However, studies have shown that acquisition of number concepts begins earlier than Piaget suggested (Ginsburg *et al.*, 1998).

As might be expected, children's understanding of the concept of conservation has been found to be influenced by the context in which it develops. So, for example, children from pottery-making families in Mexico who have fairly extensive experience of handling clay, show an understanding of conservation of mass earlier than other children (Price-Williams *et al.*, 1969).

In the following extract, Arnold (2003), in her diary documenting the development of a young child, Harry, as he progresses through the early years from birth to 5 years of age, captures in action some of the key aspects of how schemas continue to expand, and information continues to be accommodated in the later stages of Piaget's preoperational stage of cognitive development. At the time of this entry Harry was 5 years, 5 months old.

> Harry seems to want to practise holding raffles because he has only just managed to remember all the steps in the procedure. Several schemas are coordinated. A numbered ticket represents each of the participants. So, there is a 'one-to-one' correspondence between people and tickets (Athey, 1990, p. 192). Then there is a further 'one-to-one' correspondence between the tickets in the bowl and the tickets held by the participants. One set of tickets is 'spread out' or 'distributed' and the other set is 'heaped' (as in earlier 'transporting' behaviour). The sets are 'equivalent' to each other (Athey, 1990, p. 35). Numbering the tickets involves 'seriation' (Athey, 1990, p. 41). Harry is also dealing with ratios – that is if five people are participating, each has a one in five chance of winning.
>
> (2003, p. 144)

Conservation and numeracy abilities in early childhood

Developing a concept of number is one of the areas where children make substantial progress during their preschool years. When talking about a concept of number, what we mean is the awareness of how many items are present and how addition, subtraction and rearrangement affect this number (Ginsburg *et al.*, 1998). As we can see from the Piagetian conservation tasks outlined above, understanding the concept of number plays an important role in facilitating knowledge about the conservation of volume, mass and number. Kirova and Bhargava (2002) point out that the constructivist paradigm, based on Piaget's theory of cognitive development, has guided the theoretical framework for educational practice in supporting children in their acquisition of concepts through active involvement with the environment. In other words, children are provided with opportunities to construct their own knowledge through active exploration of their surroundings. With specific reference to the area of mathematics, materials can be developed and made available in early years settings that allow opportunities for young children to count, engage in active learning, and develop concepts.

We conclude this chapter with a short extract that draws attention to the invaluable contribution first-hand experiences can contribute to promoting thinking and development during the early years, as illustrated through the Reggio Emilia approach:

> These children have had repeated first-hand experiences exploring a topic actively. Their thinking about the topic is at a higher level than what Piaget would have predicted was possible for young children. Yet, if one carefully reads the documentation from the beginning of projects, one sees the type of fanciful thinking one would expect from preoperational children. It is only through the process of repeated investigations and using many different languages to represent their learning that these children begin to see the world differently and to attain higher levels of thinking about the topic.
>
> (DeMarie, 2001, np)

Implications for practice

Piaget's child in the second substage of the preoperational world continues to develop more complex abilities in their thinking, reasoning, exploring materials, engaging in mathematical thinking and much more. The child continues to initiate the activities through which they can explore and expand on their current knowledge. As they move through Piaget's preoperational stage, children are able to engage with a specified task and to apply adapted intelligence to it. Flavell (1963) also draws attention to what Piaget (1955, p. 139) termed a 'thaw out' in the 'rigid, static and irreversible structures which are typical of the early preoperational stage to thinking which has become more flexible, mobile, decentred and reversible in operation'.

1. The development of symbolic thought and representation continues throughout the preoperational stage of cognitive development. Working with children in early childhood education settings, providing resources such as sets of large and small construction toys and allowing children to explore these materials provides an excellent opportunity for children to find out, first of all, what the equipment can do and then what *they* can do with the equipment. May (2011) suggests that in this way children practise the concept of representation when, for example they use groups of families, animals and people to symbolise rainforest scenes, train stations, space adventures and so on, all the time moving towards more involved and complex scenarios.

2. Through play and informal activities preoperational children can learn about shape, size, colour, number, height, balance and structure,

as in the following documentation of activities in an early years setting:

> The children are building a structure with the cones. It is a very complex structure involving decisions about the number and spacing of cones and finding a suitable flat surface to support the next layer. The children use boxes to give the structure extra height and are very impressed and exhilarated by both the process and the end product. They work together, share ideas and combine their skills.
>
> (Brennan, 2004, p. 32)

Through these activities younger children develop their ability to describe verbally different shapes, sizes, colours and locations. These younger children also practise and consolidate their understanding of mathematical concepts such as grouping, adding and subtracting. For older children, opportunities for more advanced exploration of the concepts of gravity and balance, and more complex scientific concepts are provided through facilitating collaborative exploration in children.

3. Finding meanings through action and looking for the missing pieces in terms of explanations for what is happening in the world is central to the child in the intuitive thought substage of cognitive development. Children ask questions until they are satisfied with the answers they receive to their enquiries. Getting involved with the thinking process of the child and engaging with them in effective interactions can help them to find the appropriate language to think with, as well as effective concepts to think about (May, 2011).

4. Concepts such as the ability to compare and classify objects and to develop more complex and organised hierarchies of knowledge become central to cognitive development as children move towards the later stages of Piaget's intuitive thought substage. While Piaget did not emphasise the presence of these abilities in the preoperational stage, we know that children begin to develop these abilities in early childhood. The ability to count and classify develops across early childhood and can be supported and promoted in a variety of creative ways.

A lovely illustration of some work that tunes in to the preoperational child's exploration of classifying and categorising materials in their environments is offered in a project entitled 'the same but different', outlined by May (2011).

Children in a Midlands town in the UK were encouraged to think about and gather materials in and around the early years setting with a view to finding similarities and differences in these materials. Having collected 'treasures', the children were encouraged to classify these objects into groups either by number, shape, size or colour. However, what is emphasised is not how the classification is made but rather the skill that the children are learning. Suggestions for accompanying language include:

'That stone looks the biggest. Can you put them in order from the smallest to the biggest?'

'Are these leaves all the same green? This one looks darker to me and this one looks paler?'

5. Kirova and Bhargava (2002) draw attention to standards that emphasise that all preschool children need opportunities to explore their world and experience mathematics through play. Some of the questions that arise from this are outlined by the authors as follows:

    *   How can play and play materials enhance children's learning of primary maths concepts?
    *   As facilitators of learning, how can early years educators engage the children in activities that would enable them to further construct mathematical concepts?
    *   How can early years educators provide opportunities for each child as an individual to learn at his or her own rate?

    Play and everyday routines and experiences can provide many opportunities for young children to investigate mathematical ideas, using mathematical vocabulary and reinforcing mathematical knowledge (Stafford, 2012). Engaging with mathematical concepts through play and everyday routines and experiences helps children to develop a positive attitude to mathematics. Early years professionals facilitate learning and mathematical comprehension by assisting children's construction of knowledge in one-to-one correspondence, classification and seriation. Providing interesting resources and opportunities for children to learn about sequence and pattern, shape, space and measurement supports this learning (May, 2011).

6. The central role that language plays in supporting children's understanding of mathematical concepts is also foregrounded in some of the observations above. Kirova and Bhargava (2002) point out that in order to take Rachel from behavioural to representational knowledge, Laura was careful to use language related to the concept of matching and one-to-one correspondence. The early years professional can model the use of mathematical language and the discussion of mathematical ideas (Stafford, 2012).

Chapter 9

The concrete operational world

Piaget used the term 'concrete operations' to describe logical thinking about concrete or tangible objects and processes. In this chapter we will review and build on some of the concepts introduced in the two previous chapters and explore further. Piaget's stage of concrete operations focuses on children within the age range 7–11 years, well beyond the early years. We will focus on key Piagetian concepts associated with concrete operational thinking in order to try to clarify how thinking changes and progresses as children move through middle childhood. Piaget saw the age of 7 years as a major cognitive milestone, with the transition from preoperational to concrete operational thinking marking a turning point in cognitive development in childhood. However, more recent theorists have suggested that this transition does not involve such a significant transformation in cognitive abilities as Piaget indicated (DeHart *et al.*, 2004). It is invaluable for educators working with young children to have an understanding of how thinking develops across middle childhood and beyond, in order to support children's learning towards increasing complexity. Increasing competencies in the area of classification and seriation will be illustrated through examples from children in preschool and primary school settings. Before we go any further in exploring the details of children's cognitive development during the concrete operational stage, let's pause for a moment to consider what this term means.

What is meant by the term 'concrete operations'?

Oswalt (2010, np) below provides clarity in summarising some key features of children's thinking during this stage of concrete operations.

> A mental operation, in the Piagetian way of thinking, is the ability to accurately imagine the consequences of something happening without it actually needing to happen. During a mental operation, children imagine 'what if' scenarios which involve the imaginal transformation of mental representations of things they have experienced in the world; people, places and things. The ability to perform mental arithmetic is a

good example of an operation. Children at this age become capable of mastering addition and subtraction and similar operations and consequently are able to tell you that if they eat one cookie out of a jar containing five, that there will be four cookies left in the jar. Importantly, they can do this without actually eating a cookie and then counting the remaining cookies in the jar because they are able to model the cookie jar in their minds and operate on the contents of that mental jar so as to arrive at the answer without having to actually do the experiment.

To help us further clarify what we mean by concrete operational thinking, Wood (1998) highlights the difference between thinking that involves *mental actions* and thinking that involves *mental operations.* While mental actions involve understanding the consequences of single actions (i.e. a line of coins gets longer or shorter if we move the coins), mental operations, on the other hand, are classes of actions that are integrated with other logically related operations to form *systems* of thought and explanation. Systems of thought could also be expressed as 'mental rules' that can be applied across a number of different situations. In the concrete operational world, one such mental rule might be that 'changes in appearance may be deceptive', while another mental rule might be 'two or more sets of quantities must remain the same, if nothing is added or taken away'.

> All these aspects of understanding co-emerge as part of a system of thinking: concrete operational intelligence has been constructed.
>
> (Wood, 1998, p. 56)

One of the key features of the transition from preoperational to concrete operational thinking is that children progressively decentre and move away from an intuitive understanding of events in their worlds, to judgements based on the coordination of several acts of centration. Operations like addition and subtraction, multiplication and division become easier during this concrete operational stage (Wood, 1998). Children now have the ability to handle addition and subtraction and similar operations. However, we know from work outlined in previous chapters that these abilities have been developing through the early years and it is within this concrete operational stage that they become refined and further developed. The dialogue between Elisa (7 years old) and Jack (6 years old) illustrates this, as they work on a jigsaw puzzle together:

ELISA: Ok, that piece is good here. How many more pieces do we need to finish?

JACK: (counting spaces) One, two, three, four, five . . . five pieces we need.

ELISA: Five pieces . . . ok, let's find five pieces . . . but it can't be five . . . there are only 3 pieces left so there must be two pieces missing.

Elisa is very comfortable in working out how many pieces are missing – she can handle the subtraction operation with ease when she quickly subtracts 3 from 5 to get the missing two pieces. What is interesting is that Elisa is able to work this operation out in her head. She does not need to physically count the 3 pieces from the 5 pieces, but can calculate this operation mentally and come up with the right answer. These strategies and systems of thought are called *concrete* because children can only apply them to immediately present objects. As children's representations are limited to objects or events that are tangible and concrete, so children's understanding and knowledge about the consequences of events is more concrete in scope.

We have seen children plan and carry out actions throughout the preoperational stage. What we see develop in the concrete operational stage is children's growing ability to imagine the consequences of their actions, without actually having to carry out those actions. In an interesting article entitled 'Revealing the work of young engineers in early childhood education', the differences between children's thinking in the preoperational stage and older children's thinking as they approach concrete operational thought is well illustrated (Van Meeteren & Zan, 2010, np):

> In the children's technical creation of ramp structures, they gradually come to understand their structure as a series of subsystems and that making an adjustment in one subsystem will affect others. Evidence that children do not yet see their structure as a system can be seen, for example, when 3-year-olds shift one end of a segment of cove moulding to the left or right so that it will align with the next segment. But shifting one end of the segment causes the other end to shift in the opposite direction. Preschoolers are frequently surprised and perplexed by this, and only after experiencing it several times do they begin to recognize when it will happen.

The younger children in the early stages of preoperational thinking are focusing on one aspect of the construction, working hard to align one segment of the construction with another. However, as yet they are not able to carry out the mental operation that signals that if you shift one piece of wood in a particular direction, another piece will move in the opposite direction. Only having actually carried out the action several times will some of the children in the preoperational stage understand the consequences of their actions. Let's return to see how this construction proceeds.

> Evidence of systems thinking can be seen, for example, in children's efforts to get a marble to turn a corner (something that most children attempt at some point in the design process). One solution to the corner problem is to elevate the starting end of the first ramp and then place a block at the end to allow the marble to ricochet onto the next ramp. If

the force of the marble onto the ricochet block is too great, the marble's trajectory will be off the second ramp. Success requires the coordination of the first ramp's degree of incline with the position of the block and second ramp. That is, the child can lower the incline, thus slowing the marble down so that it does not strike the ricochet block with as much force, and bounces gently onto the second ramp.

The older children are able to stand back and use concrete operational thinking to work out that if they adjust the incline of the first ramp, they can ensure that the marble does not strike the ricochet block with too much force, so that it can eventually arrive in the second ramp.

The journey from preoperational to concrete operational thinking

A number of very important changes and improvements in children's cognitive abilities become apparent in the transition from preoperational thinking to cognitive operational thinking. Some of these changes include:

- Ability to engage in more systematic and logical thinking, helped along by the child's increasing ability to decentre – to focus on more than one aspect of an event.
- Ability to be able to discriminate between superficial appearance and the underlying reality. As children begin to grasp the concept of conservation of number, mass, weight and volume, they are better able to tell the difference between what appears to be happening and what is actually happening.
- Knowledge and understanding of the environment becomes domain-specific, allowing children to build expertise in a very particular area of their experience.
- Attention and memory abilities become more refined and selective.

These abilities are illustrated in the following extract, where we see Nicole in the later stages of the preoperational world planning and constructing her house:

> Nicole has commandeered a box. First, she struggles with fitting the box under the table and then with manoeuvring the box to face outwards. She stays with it and succeeds. Next she inveigles the help of Donnagh as he passes by. 'Will you hold this for a minute?' He obliges. She gets two chairs carrying both together and skilfully uses her whole body to manoeuvre these into place. Her sense of space and size tells her that these two chairs should fit in the box and they do – just perfectly.
>
> (Brennan 2004, p. 6)

Nicole is learning about size, space, density, supporting structures, manoeuvrability – she can think about an action and whether it will work or not, without having to carry out the action in advance. Many of the concepts that become refined and more sophisticated in the concrete operational world have already begun to emerge in the preoperational world. In the following sections we briefly revisit these emerging competencies.

Conservation

The concept of conservation was introduced in earlier chapters. Children's ability to understand the concept of conservation develops and refines across middle childhood and is associated with the development of the following constructs:

Decentration: attending to more than one feature of an event or action.
Reversibility of thought or mentally reversing an action: understanding that certain logical operations, such as addition, can be reversed by others, such as subtraction.
Transitive inference: the ability to logically combine relations in order to reach a conclusion. We will return to this later in this chapter.

One of the limitations in the thinking patterns of younger preoperational children was that their understanding of what was happening in events tended to be influenced exclusively by what they *perceived* to be happening, rather than by the reality of the situation. As we have pointed out a number of times, appearance tends to win out over the reality of a situation for the younger child. Although they have witnessed nothing being added or taken away from a quantity, they perceive there to be more liquid in one glass because that glass is taller than the original one and this perception influences their understanding of a situation.

So, children in the concrete operational stage of cognitive development have learned to overcome what we have termed the appearance–reality problem.

Julie (7 years old) is waiting in line before going back inside after playing outdoors in the school grounds. As the children are waiting in line, some children move sideways and the line becomes curved around and snaking. When asked to move into a straight line, the line now appears to become longer. Julie knows, however, that although the line appears longer, in fact, the number of children in the line has remained the same, and it will, therefore, take the same amount of time for her to reach the entrance to the building.

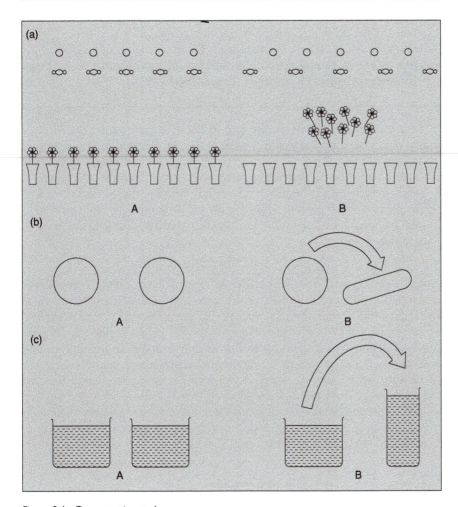

Figure 9.1. Conservation tasks

Children are no longer deceived by superficial appearance as, for example, when the same amount of water in a short, fat glass looks more when it is poured into a long, skinny glass. Piaget estimated that conservation of number is achieved first at about 5 or 6 years of age, followed by conservation of mass at around 7 or 8 years of age and conservation of liquid is fully understood around 10 or 11 years of age (Fisher & Bullock, 1984).

Figure 9.1 above provides a visual summary of the kinds of tasks associated with the different concepts of conservation.

For Piaget, two distinct kinds of knowledge were necessary in order to achieve an understanding of conservation.

Contingent truth: This kind of knowledge is based on what we observe to be true – what we perceive to be happening around us.

Necessary truth: This kind of knowledge is based on logical necessity and the processing of mental operations, apart from the information gathered through the senses (Inhelder & Piaget, 1964).

Susie (3 years, 5 months) is spinning round with her eyes closed. When she opens her eyes, the world continues to spin, she sees her house spin around her and she becomes frightened as this is not a very pleasant experience. Susie is responding based on contingent truth – the reality she is perceiving through her senses, but without the constraint of a necessary truth that would let her know that houses do not spin around and that the sensation is due to the fact that she, herself, has been spinning round.

Piaget believed that the acquisition of the skill to conserve properties developed in children as a result of the same logical skills that allowed them to understand conservation across all of the different situations above. However, we know there is what Piaget himself termed a horizontal décalage (developmental lag) in terms of how these skills emerge. In simpler terms, a horizontal décalage refers to the fact that children understand conservation of number before they understand conservation of liquid. Piaget believed such a décalage occurred because children may be experiencing the physical world in different contexts – social, cultural, educational – and these contexts may furnish some children with opportunities to explore the properties of materials sooner than other children.

Sequence of understanding conservation

According to Piaget, children's understanding of the concept of conservation develops fully in middle childhood (e.g. from 6 years of age onwards). Piaget also highlighted the fact that children do not develop an understanding of these different concepts of conservation all at once, but develop an understanding of these different concepts at different times. DeHart *et al.* (2004) provide an insightful account of the different stages through which children's thinking evolves in order to fully grasp the concept of conservation of liquid volume. In this account they highlight the tendency of these young children to mistake superficial appearance for reality when they focus only on one aspect of the process they are watching.

Stage 1: (3- and 4-year-olds)

In this stage of understanding, children are *non-conservers*. They consistently judge the amount of liquid by its height alone. Non-conservers tend to rely on a particular rule to the exclusion of other information that is relevant to a more complete understanding. They rely on this consistent rule to make evaluations about the amount – the higher the level of liquid, the more liquid there is. During this stage, children seem very certain and quite content that they are correct in their evaluations.

Stage 2 (5- and 6-year-olds)

In this stage children enter a transitional period in terms of their understanding of the conservation of volume. During this period, they tend to become less decisive and certain about their evaluation of whether the volume of liquid remains the same or has increased across the transformation of appearances. They may first of all say the taller glass has more liquid but may also wonder if the other has more because it is wider. And they may be able to give consideration to the fact that if the water was poured back into the original glass, the amount would again be equal. DeHart *et al.* (2004) point out that during this stage, children's uncertainty can be explained by the fact that they can now bring more information to their understanding of conservation.

Stage 3: (7 years and over)

This stage is known as *mature conservation* and children tend to answer the questions asked quickly, confidently and correctly. For these children the answer is obvious and they might judge the responses of younger children to be silly. This ability is one of the cognitive markers for the transition into middle childhood. One of the following four justifications for answers is typically provided by children in this stage.

Compensation: 'This one is higher but it's narrower; the other one is shorter, but it's wider. So they're both the same.'
Reversibility: 'When you pour it back, it will be the same again.'
Identity: 'It's still the same water.'
The nothing added or subtracted criterion: 'You only poured it into a different glass.'

So a number of key points are worth thinking about when we try to capture some of the key features and abilities that are associated with children's ability to understand conservation.

- While preschool children in the preoperational stage of cognitive development are able to succeed on certain aspects of tasks of conservation, these abilities become refined during the concrete operational stage (from 7 years of age onwards).
- Children are able to explain their responses to such tasks using what has been termed explanations based on necessary truth.
- Children in the concrete operational stage, with a firm understanding of the concept of conservation, are well equipped to perform on many primary school maths and arithmetic tasks.
- Children in middle childhood and in the concrete operational stage of cognitive development demonstrate significant improvement in *metacognition* – the ability to think effectively about their own knowledge and processes of thought.

Deductive reasoning

Goswami defines human reasoning as 'mental activity that involves the manipulation of given information to reach new conclusions' (2011, p. 399). The author goes on to distinguish between two major types of reasoning: inductive reasoning and deductive reasoning. Inductive reasoning involves using specific information or knowledge to generalise about something – for example, we can remember back to the genius of babies who in their first years were able to induce from specific situations to more general realities. An example of inductive reasoning in these cases was learning from banging a spoon on a tin box that when you hit a hard object with a hard object it makes a loud noise.

Deductive reasoning, on the other hand, involves deducing a new piece of information from information already provided. One aspect of deductive reasoning is transitive inference – inferring new information about someone or something based on information provided about the relationship between these people or objects.

Piaget believed that children acquire the ability to use transitive reasoning in the concrete operational stage of cognitive development around 6 or 7 years of age. However, later research suggested that preoperational children may not be able to draw transitive inferences due to a memory deficit rather than limitation in logical reasoning. When younger children, aged 4 and 5 years, were trained to memorise key information, these children were found to be able to engage in transitive inference (Phillips *et al.*, 2009). Significantly, Goswami (2011) draws attention to the fact that children's ability to engage in deductive reasoning is strongly influenced by the nature and context in which the problem is located. In other words, once children are reasonably familiar with the concepts they are exploring, they are better able to engage in both inductive and deductive reasoning tasks.

Hierarchical classification

Piaget also highlighted the increased development of children's ability to categorise and classify information during the concrete operational stage of cognitive development. In previous chapters, we noted that children's ability to classify things in a basic way begins very early in childhood. Children can tidy away books, blocks, puzzles and various toys into the different places they belong, which tells us that they are able to categorise and sort things in a fundamental way by 3–4 years of age. Children in middle childhood go beyond these abilities and can engage in more complex, hierarchical classification, organising concepts into levels of abstraction that can range from very specific (e.g. dog) to the very general (e.g. animals) (Hetherington & Parke, 2003). The ability to classify things hierarchically continues to develop across the concrete operational stage between the ages of 7 and 10 years. These improved abilities in performing hierarchical classification are very significant for young children as they are increasingly faced with scientific concepts in school settings. Being able to make comparisons and categorisations, as, for example, sorting living creatures into different groups based on whether they are animals or plants, is very useful to children.

Let's consider some of these abilities in action in the following examples from 'A trip to the zoo: children's words and photographs', in which DeMarie (2001) observed and documented some of the similarities and differences in observations, perceptions and priorities across children aged 3–12 years, from early preoperational worlds to concrete operational worlds.

- Over 80% of children aged 6–12 years took photographs that contained animals in comparison with only 56% of the younger children.
- Children in the preoperational stage were more likely to photograph familiar animals (e.g. chipmunks), whereas children in the concrete operational stage took photographs of a range of animals and included rare animals such as a red panda.
- Children in the concrete operational stage noticed and learned new features of familiar animals and also about new, unfamiliar animals.
- Children in the preoperational stage were more likely to photograph action (e.g. swimming, petting animals). These young children also photographed the clouds, ground and other items not uniquely associated with the zoo.
- Children in the preoperational stage seemed to need more than one exposure to unfamiliar phenomena to notice and to remember them.
- Only the children in the later stage of concrete operations (e.g. 10–12 years of age) indicated that they understood abstract concepts such as the need to conserve animals.

Seriation

A related ability that further develops throughout the concrete operational stage of cognitive development is being able to order material in a series, according to its quantity or magnitude. A pre-requisite of this ability to seriate is the ability to count. Seriation skills are fundamental to children's understanding of school subjects, especially with regard to maths and science. However, as we have noted before, in their everyday lives, children use basic seriation skills to order their toys, as, for example, when children organise their toys from smallest to largest. We had a clear illustration of seriation abilities in an earlier extract by Kirova and Bhargava (2002) in which Rachel was able to allocate the appropriate sized teddy to the role of 'papa bear' and 'baby bear', and Tiffany who, with ease, was able to select the smallest spoon for the baby bear and the largest spoon for the 'papa bear', further demon-strating a basic understanding of ordering things from smallest to largest. Arnold draws our attention to the many instances of children's emerging ability to seriate in the early years, when documenting the development of Harry (5 years, 5 months):

> Harry talked about Grandad looking older than a man at the Community Centre, who is 70; Grandad and Grandpop being about the same size; me being fatter than Nana (he said 'She is very thin'). I said something about my living room being small. He said 'Mummy's room is bigger than this' and 'Daddy's room is definitely bigger than yours'.
>
> (2010, p. 100)

As children move through Piaget's concrete operational stage of cognitive development, they are frequently called on to use their seriation skills in more complex ways in formal school contexts, particularly in material related to maths and science subjects.

Attention and memory

Two important features of the transition from preoperational to concrete operational thinking involve a significant improvement in children's attention and memory skills. As we have seen in previous chapters, children progressively move away from an exclusive focus on one aspect of an event or activity and develop the ability to integrate information from a number of sources simultaneously. A number of studies have supported this development, with a more detailed focus on the development of children's ability to attend to information increasingly across early childhood and into middle childhood.

Miller (1990) carried out an interesting study that compared 4-year-olds' abilities to attend to and scan information with the abilities of older children

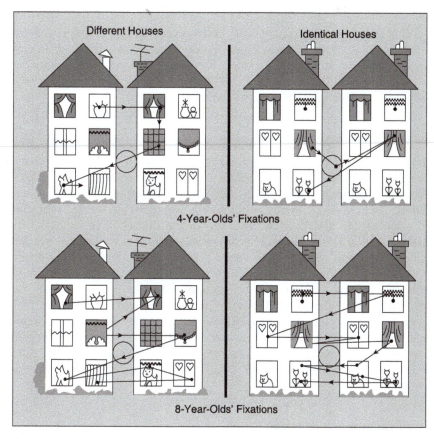

Figure 9.2. Attention and scanning patterns of children aged 4 years and 8 years of age

of 8 years of age. Young children tend to scan more information than they need to solve a particular task. Children were shown 12 pictures, 6 of animals and 6 of household objects. The pictures were arranged on a board with 12 windows, one picture inside each window.

Children were asked to remember only the animal pictures. Older children tended to open only the windows covering the animal pictures. Preschoolers, on the other hand, did not use this selective behaviour and failed to direct their attention in an organised and effective way. These younger children chose to open all windows rather than just the windows with animals behind (Miller, 1990). Figure 9.2 above also illustrates scanning patterns of 4- and 8-year-old children when asked to identify similarities and differences in pairs of houses.

Transition from preschool to primary school

> The implication of seeing child development as a series of progressive psychological transformations, from one stage to the next, from infancy to maturity, is that these stages become crucial reference points for discussing optimal timing for transitions, e.g., from home to preschool or from more informal to more formal curriculum.
>
> (Vogler *et al.*, 2008, p. 5)

Many children experience the transition to formal schooling during what might be termed the 'cusp' between the preoperational and the concrete operational world. Piaget provides us with a greater understanding of how thinking develops and changes as children move from early childhood into middle childhood. These observations help us understand the need for staff to acknowledge and build on the knowledge that children have already gained in order to support each child's development as a capable learner. We have seen that as children move from preoperational thinking to concrete operational thinking, they are able to process complex information more effectively, going beyond the surface appearance of things to focus on multiple aspects of an event. However, we have emphasised throughout this book that Piaget's theory tends to overestimate the extent to which children's development is universal and we know that the key to more successful transitions from preschool to primary school involves supporting each child individually with regard to their cognitive and other abilities (Fabian & Dunlop, 2007).

Implications for practice

Much of the material we have outlined in this chapter focuses on children beyond early childhood. Clearly, the implications for working with young children are less obvious when we consider this later stage of development. In the following sections, we will focus on a small number of key messages that emerge from reflection on cognitive development during Piaget's concrete operational stage with a view to helping us understand how we can best support children's cognitive development during the transition from preschool to primary school and beyond.

- When we consider children's thinking in Piaget's concrete operational stage of cognitive development, we can see the progression from understanding based on concrete and actual experiences to more abstract, mental reasoning. The benefits for children of promoting cognitive development through preschool activities is evidenced in findings from the EPPE study (Sylva *et al.*, 2004), which indicate that there are significant differences in children's cognitive development between children who have attended preschool and, in particular, high-quality preschool when compared with children who have not had such experiences. The benefits of high-quality preschool provision on cognitive development in childhood are evident up to 7 years of age.

- The importance for children's learning of interactions with the physical, concrete world around them is once again emphasised in Piaget's concrete operational stage. Although children are now better able to use mental operations in terms of processing and making sense of the world around them, the ongoing need to facilitate opportunities for children to handle and explore is highlighted in Piaget's theory. Children continue to build on their knowledge of objects and to become more familiar with the specific properties of these objects when they are provided with situations that generate opportunities for learning in the real world.

- Providing opportunities for promoting systematic and 'joined up' thinking in children is emphasised in Piaget's concrete operational stage of development. The importance of creating environments that allow children to engage in planning, designing and constructing has been highlighted in research on children's emerging abilities in middle childhood. In line with Piaget's constructivist principles, such opportunities not only provide opportunities for improving mathematical and scientific competencies in early and middle childhood but also promote and support possibilities for children to develop socio-emotional skills through negotiating, decision-making and developing consensus. Stimulating learning through field studies and immersion in experiences allows for the emergence of understandings to occur as students physically interact with each other and their environment.

- In Piaget's concrete operational stage, we see the development of domain-specific expertise in children. In other words, children become expert in areas of particular interest to them. However, we know that these abilities are developing through the preoperational stage of development. The importance of encouraging younger children to develop their interests and the corresponding abilities to support these interests is an important message that we can bring from the concrete operational world to working with younger children. An illustration of younger children's interests and expertise is provided in the following observation where Jack is creating a sun to include in a mural being made collaboratively by children in his preschool setting:

> Jack is a powerful learner. He displays an amazing ability to self organise and self regulate. He is focused, persistent and takes pride in his work. These are all the characteristics of the high achiever. They are the learning dispositions that we, as childcare workers, want to support.
>
> (Brennan, 2004, p. 10)

- The concepts of classification, conservation, seriation and one-to-one correspondence are fundamental to understanding and working with mathematical concepts as children move through middle childhood within more formal schooling contexts. We know that these concepts begin to emerge in early childhood and are further refined through the late preoperational stage and concrete operational stage of cognitive development. The importance of continuing to facilitate discovery learning for children in this stage of cognitive development is highlighted by Edwards and Knight (2001), who suggest helping young children to work through mathematical concepts by actively measuring aspects of a classroom, with educators directing students' attention to salient features and away from irrelevant features.

Chapter 10

The formal operational world

As we begin to think about Piaget's final stage of cognitive development – formal operational thinking – we become aware of how we have travelled a long distance from thinking in early childhood. In this final stage of cognitive development, Piaget drew attention to the centrality of abstract, logical and idealistic thinking. This chapter will provide an overview of some of the key developments within this stage of development, which Piaget believed began around 11 years of age. The young person's thinking is abstract in the sense that they can mentally manipulate information without needing to rely on the concrete presence of this information. Adolescent thinking is logical in that young people can systematically test alternative solutions to a problem. Piaget called this kind of thinking hypothetical-deductive reasoning – the ability to hypothesise, to hold in mind a number of imagined possibilities and to draw conclusions based on these mental experiments. Thinking in the formal operational world is clearly qualitatively different to the young child's thinking in early and middle childhood. A focus on this stage of cognitive development allows us greater insight into how our thinking as adults is often at a remove from children's thinking. Moreover, an understanding of the stages of progression from infancy to adolescent thinking contributes to how we can support and enhance thinking and development in early childhood.

Overview of formal operational world

According to Piaget, formal operational thinking is achieved approximately between the ages of 11 and 15 years. Perhaps the most significant feature of this kind of thinking according to Piaget's theory is that we are no longer reliant on the concrete world in order to imagine, reflect on and draw conclusions about events in the world around us. If we think back to chapter 5, we described the concept of object permanence. Object permanence is the ability to understand that objects exist even though we can no longer see them. Piaget illustrated this concept through detailed observations of his infant daughter Jacqueline and her responses to the disappearance of the rubber duck that Piaget was playing with in front of her.

So, we began this book about Piaget's stages of cognitive development with descriptions of very brilliant babies who managed to make sense of a world that was an ever-changing feast of magical occurrences, but whose ability to understand was confined to the here and now – the concrete, physical world of movement and sensations. Below we focus on some of the key features of formal operational thought.

Hypothetical reasoning

In the formal operational world, the young adolescent can conjure up their own world through imagination and hypothesis. Formal operational thinking involves the ability to consider hypothetical possibilities and to reason logically about these possibilities. Moving further away from the need to test things out in the concrete world, thinking in the formal operational world involves being able to consider the logical relations among several possibilities or to deduce conclusions from abstract statements (Smith *et al.*, 2003).

In Piaget's formal operational stage of cognitive development, we can ponder endless possibilities and consequences without ever having to engage with the actions that bring about these consequences. Piaget refers to this kind of thought as hypothetical deductive reasoning (Santrock, 2011). In other words, young people can now think about problems in a more scientific way through developing plans to solve problems and systematically testing the possible solutions to a problem in order to identify the best possibility.

Idealism

Related to this development of the ability to consider endless possibilities and probabilities is the ability to think about things in an idealistic manner. When you can think more effectively about the consequences of an action – including the moral consequences of your behaviour – it is possible to develop more refined and complex ideal standards that can guide behaviour and thought. One of the significant developments associated with formal operational thinking is being able to reflect on your own character and to aspire towards ideal characteristics. In the formal operational world, the individual can compare themselves with many others and, thereby, adjust and alter their behaviour to fit in with their conception of an ideal self.

Self and identity

Piaget's description of cognitive development in adolescence links in with other theories of adolescence, such as Erikson's stages of psychosocial development where the achievement of identity is foregrounded as a major milestone in adolescence. The ability to think about yourself and to compare yourself with others, in terms of your abilities, contributes to the development of a sense of self and identity. In early childhood, children tend to describe themselves and others in concrete terms. For example, they may focus on physical features such as hair colour, height and ability to run fast. As they move through middle childhood in the concrete operational stage of development, children become better able to describe themselves in abstract terms, referring to internal states and qualities (Hetherington & Parke, 2003). In the formal operational period the young person can think about themselves drawing on more abstract qualities and being able to coordinate and integrate somewhat contradictory qualities.

A return to egocentrism

We have come across the term egocentrism many times throughout Piaget's stages of cognitive development. From the beginning, we noted that infants are egocentric in their early behaviours and become better able to take the perspective of others as they move through the preoperational stage of cognitive development. Through the sensorimotor, preoperational and concrete operational stages, children become less egocentric and develop the ability to decentre – to focus on several aspects of an event simultaneously. We have also seen how children progressively develop the ability to take the perspectives of others and are able to better understand other people's thought, desires and beliefs. Formal operational thought provides young people with the ability to imagine what other people might be thinking and how they might behave in certain situations. Paradoxically, this increasing ability in the formal operational world to understand what others might be thinking or feeling in a particular situation may contribute to the concept of adolescent egocentrism (Elkind, 1967).

It is important for us to distinguish between the term egocentrism as it is used in early childhood and in adolescence. In contrast to the egocentric thinking of the toddler and preschooler, adolescent egocentrism does not mean that the adolescent cannot take the perspective of others – it simply means that with the ability to think in a more complex way about the self and others' perspectives on the self, young people become more self-conscious, tending to focus their attention on themselves.

Metacognition

Metacognition is the process of reflecting on thought itself. In the formal operational world, young people develop the ability to think more effectively about what they are thinking and are better able to evaluate and monitor their own thought processes (Edwards & Knight, 2001). These abilities begin in early childhood and can be supported through encouraging young children to set goals in their learning, to self-monitor and self-evaluate the achievement of those goals in programmes such as HighScope and Reggia Emilia. The ability to monitor cognitive processes in terms of developing flexible and effective strategies to increase cognitive performance are key features of thinking in the formal operational world.

Formal operational tasks

Throughout all the stages of Piaget's theory of cognitive development, abilities are measured using specific tasks that Piaget designed to assess the different cognitive competencies he was exploring. One example of a task that assesses formal operational thinking is the rather difficult and complex pendulum task (Inhelder & Piaget, 1958) (see Figure 10.1 over- leaf). Individuals are given a string that can be shortened or lengthened along with a set of weights and asked to identify what determines the speed of swing of the pendulum – the length of the string, the weight at the end of the string, the height at which the weight is released or how forcefully the weight is pushed (Smith *et al.*, 2003). One of the major characteristics of this thinking is the ability to scientifically consider different possibilities and to draw logical deductions from trials with different combinations of materials. Adolescents using formal operations consider all of the factors that might be responsible for possible combinations, reasoning that any one factor could be responsible for the speed of the pendulum's swing. They then systematically test each factor one at a time, holding the other factors constant, until they arrive at the correct solution (Cook & Cook, 2008).

From concrete experience to scientific deduction

As with many of the stages of cognitive development that we have been focusing on in this book, Piaget saw the formal operational world as developing over time. In his earlier writings, Piaget suggested that most of the milestones within the formal operational period were achieved between the ages of 12 and 15 years (Hetherington & Parke, 2003). However, he later revised his thinking to conclude that formal operational thinking is not achieved entirely until between approximately 15 and 20 years of age. More recent research suggests that the achievement of formal operational thinking may be more gradual than Piaget indicated and may also be dependent on the nature of the tasks involved (Smith *et al.*, 2003). It has also been suggested that formal operational thinking may only be used some of the time and in domains that we are familiar with.

   It is interesting at this point to pause and reflect a little on how the child has progressed through Piaget's early stages of sensorimotor cognitive development, to thought that becomes less reliant on physical reality and is increasingly underpinned by symbolic representation in the preoperational

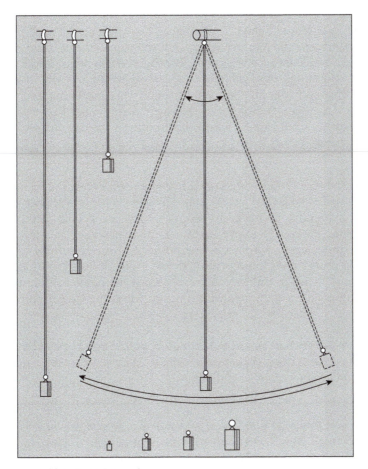

Figure 10.1. Pendulum task

stage of cognitive development. In the concrete operational world, children extend these abilities and develop abilities to reason systematically. Finally, in this formal operational world, young people can ponder real-life experiences without ever having to engage in these experiences. So, while we saw that interacting with the physical world and playing with objects and peers was central to learning and development in the early stages of Piaget's theory, knowledge now draws on mental operations and the development of abstract conceptual knowledge (Smidt, 2009).

To remind ourselves of the voyage from sensorimotor learning in infancy all the way to formal operational thinking in adolescence, let's observe some younger children in activities in Piaget's sensorimotor and early preoperational stages of cognitive development.

> Kaylie, a 2-year-old child, is playing on the kitchen floor with plastic lids, containers and measuring cups. For some time, she has been trying to place a blue lid on a clear container. At a certain point, Kaylie picks up a measuring cup and moves the blue lid to rest on its open end. However, the blue lid cannot rest on the measuring cup's rim because the open end of the cup is larger than the lid. Kaylie pauses. Then she lets the blue lid fall to the bottom of the cup and presses it down firmly.

Forman and Hall (2005) suggest that Kaylie pauses because she wants to find a way to make the lid rest on the cup. However, when she realises that this strategy is not going to work, she adjusts her goal to become 'fitting the lid' somewhere. Kaylie's cognitive activity is determined by her interactions with the immediate environment around her and she is learning to understand the properties of objects through her explorations of touching them. In contrast to older children, however, Kaylie may not be able to think about altering her strategy to achieve her aim. However, she adjusts her goals to fit in with what she can achieve through her explorations with physical properties.

Kaylie's solitary but intense concentration on finding a resting place for the lid contrasts with the preoperational child's ability to negotiate a shared set of rules and roles with other children.

> Aoife and Reece are both 4 years old and love to play with water. Reece uses plastic tubing and a bottle to make what he calls 'a volcano'. He is learning that he can displace water by blowing air into the bottle. He learns also that, at a given point, he is unable to displace any more water and must refill in order to repeat his feat. Aoife is eager to have a try and tells Reece that he has had five goes 'one, two, three, four, five', and she holds up five fingers in front of his face. Aoife is then given a chance to try it out (Brennan, 2004, p. 4).

Reece and Aoife are developing knowledge and understanding of concepts such as volume, capacity, force, displacement and their knowledge can be reinforced and extended through conversation and discussion around these experiences (Brennan, 2004).

In contrast to children and young people in the later concrete and formal operational stages of development, these younger children test out their hypotheses through *acting on* the world around them.

Concrete operational world and formal operational world

One of the major differences between children's problem-solving abilities in the concrete operational world and the formal operational world is that the adolescent can solve problems even if they are mentally represented, whereas the child in the concrete operational period can only solve problems when the objects are actually present. A very good illustration of such abilities is provided by findings from a task devised by Inhelder and Piaget (1958). In this task children are asked to think of reasons to explain why some objects float and why other objects do not float, using a variety of objects and water to explore this phenomenon. Younger children found it difficult to grasp the more abstract concepts such as mass and density in contrast to the older participants who had a basic understanding of abstract concepts.

Children who are in the concrete operational stage of cognitive development base their solutions on the observable characteristics of size and weight and are unable to consider alternatives not directly observable in the physical world (Hetherington & Parke, 2003). These children tend to focus on weight or size as a reason for why things sink or float. In the formal operational world, however, the young person can think about a number of possible alternatives in order to arrive at the concept of density in explaining the phenomenon.

What have we learned about the formal operational world since Piaget?

As we have seen throughout this book, while Piaget's theory of cognitive development has been invaluable in guiding our understanding of how thinking and cognition progresses through childhood and adolescence, more recent research has established that Piaget was not always accurate in his beliefs about the timing and sequence of these cognitive abilities. While Piaget emphasised maturation and biological processes as being central to the development of cognitive abilities, other researchers have demonstrated that the achievement of formal operational thinking may be more dependent on the context that supports this development and on the nature of the task that assesses these competencies (Smith *et al.*, 2003). Moreover, the achievement of formal operational thinking may be limited to certain domains only. Young people and adults may be more likely to achieve the capacity for logical abstract reasoning within their particular areas of interest or expertise.

As an illustration of these critiques, more recent research in the UK has shown that when given the pendulum task, only about 30% of 16-year-old schoolchildren had achieved 'early formal operations' (Shayer & Wylam, 1978). Other studies have indicated that not all children reach formal operational thinking in their teenage years. The importance of culture and context has also been highlighted with regard to the achievement of formal operational thinking, similar to learning and development across all Piaget's cognitive stages.

Implications for education

- The implications of Piaget's formal operational stage of cognitive development are best considered in terms of their relevance to education at secondary and higher levels (Smith *et al.*, 2003). In mathematics and science lessons at primary school, children are helped to make the transition from preoperational thinking to concrete operations through carefully arranged sequences of experiences that develop an understanding, for example, of class inclusion, conservation and perspective-taking. At a later period, the teacher can encourage practical and experimental work before moving on to abstract deductive reasoning. In this way, the teacher can provide the conditions that are appropriate for the transition from concrete operational thinking to the stage of formal operational thinking.
- The central role of the young person's active engagement in their own learning is further highlighted in the formal operational stage of cognitive development. Educators can maximise opportunities for self-directed learning, motivated by the unremitting curiosity of the young learner in adolescence. Young people develop increasing abilities to monitor and reflect critically on their own learning strategies as they move through the formal operational stage of cognitive development.

Chapter 11

Drawing it all together

Introduction

What does Piaget's theory of cognitive development contribute to our understanding of young children's thinking and development? How can we draw on the concepts and principles of Piaget's theory to develop a solid pedagogy for professionals working with children in the early years? Does children's play in infancy and the early years reflect the features of young children's thinking as outlined by Piaget? This chapter will draw together some of the key ideas and concepts introduced in previous chapters. Specifically, the chapter will summarise key principles in the progression from sensorimotor infant thinking through more symbolic and intuitive thinking in early childhood. Case studies will be used to illustrate and synthesise key abilities and competencies within these stages of development. The emergence of logical thinking and its refinement through middle childhood to abstract thinking in adolescence will also be synthesised and illustrated through the development of case studies, applying these theoretical concepts to children's activities and interactions in the real world. Key issues relevant to a pedagogy for early childhood education are captured in this final chapter with a view to providing guidance for students and practitioners to follow up on the knowledge that has been generated by Piaget's followers. We explore the many ways in which Piagetian principles and concepts can be effectively applied to working creatively to support and enhance children's learning and development.

What does Piaget's theory of cognitive development contribute to our understanding of young children's thinking and development in early childhood?

Piaget's contribution to our understanding of development in the early years and beyond cannot be over-emphasised. When asked which theorists they felt most strongly influenced their approach to early childhood education, early childhood practitioners in the USA cited Piaget as having the most predominant influence on their approach, while Vygotsky followed close behind (Hyson *et al.*, 2009). Similarly, practitioners highlighted constructivism as one of the key theories shaping educational approaches in this study. It is interesting that so many years after his theory was developed, Piaget's ideas still play a major role in influencing educational practices.

In the following sections we pause to think further about Piaget's main contributions to our understanding of how cognitive abilities develop through infancy and childhood. These contributions are summarised briefly under broad headings as follows: a tangible sense of thinking in childhood, concepts in childhood, cycles of adaptation, stages of thinking and understanding, and active, child-motivated learning.

Tangible sense of thinking in childhood

Working closely with young children provides many opportunities to observe the rich and subtle development that takes place in children's minds across these early years. Piaget's theory provided us with unprecedented foundational and concrete knowledge on which to build educational approaches and practice. As Siegler expresses it, 'Piaget's theory conveys an almost tangible sense of what children's thinking is like . . .' (1991, p. 18). It is this quality – a tangible sense of children's thinking – that has allowed research and practice in the early years to build and expand on knowledge of children's thinking and how we can plan to work with children in an effective and meaningful way. This might involve watching the young child build their understanding of object permanence, seeing the toddler develop and expand on a schema for lifting objects, observing children expand on their expression through their use of symbolic representation, hearing the preschooler question the reason why shadows grow longer as we move from morning to afternoon. Piaget identified and drew further attention to some of the most interesting features of children's thinking and how that thinking changes over time.

We know that Piaget has been criticised for the limitations in aspects of his theory of cognitive development. However, despite the prolific attempts to critique, dissemble and often reject the contribution that Piaget made to our understanding of cognitive development in childhood and beyond, his legacy is undeniable and well summed up in the following extract from John Flavell.

> Piaget provided the field with an entirely new vision of the nature of children, and of the what, when, and how of their cognitive growth. This vision invaded the field during the 1960s and 1970s and largely supplemented the rather limited and uninteresting visions that were already there.
>
> (1996, p. 200)

Concepts in childhood

A very positive contribution of Piaget's theory was the insight it provided us with regard to when and how children develop certain concepts during the early years and beyond. In addition to providing insight, in a general sense, into the nature and texture of children's thinking at different stages of their development, Piaget drew attention to the detail of their abilities even at the pre-verbal stage. We know that Piaget may have underestimated the age at which these concepts are achieved, but in general we know that the sequence in which they are achieved has remained unchanged since Piaget's theory. As Miller (2010) points out, Piaget's claims generated much thought about and research into what it means to have a concept. In his desire not to misrepresent or over-estimate the presence of ability, Piaget made heavy demands within his tasks.

More generally, concepts such as egocentrism, centration and decentration, and the guidelines Piaget's theory provided in the timing and emergence of these concepts, continue to be very useful in providing early childhood practitioners with a baseline from which to develop strategies to support and promote the development of such concepts. We know, for example, that there have been many challenges to Piaget's views on egocentrism in childhood and these challenges, in turn, have generated fascinating experiments that suggest that Piaget underestimated the rational powers of young children at times (Donaldson, 1978; Perner et al., 1987; Young-Ihm, 2002).

Cycles of adaptation

Piaget's theory emphasises the cyclical nature of the acquisition of knowledge – a spiral-like progression – based on adaptation and adjustment to new information in the environment. Recall chapter 1, where we saw an ongoing process of experience, reflection on that experience and continuous updating of mental representations of the world in order to make that representation more accurate. Early childhood educators play a central role in sequencing learning experiences and in supporting the accommodation process of the child (Edwards & Knight, 2001). As we have seen, the building blocks of cognitive development for Piaget are assimilation and accommodation – complementary processes that facilitate adaptation. In the following extract, the cyclical pattern of learning and adaptation is well captured:

> A child playing with wet sand – sometimes simply enjoying the sensation of damp roughness, sometimes repeating rituals of chugging a bulldozer along smooth pathways, sometimes making tunnels and beginning to get a sense of how long a tunnel can be in proportion to its width and the amount of sand around it – is not simply either assimilating or

accommodating. She or he is doing each in turn. Assimilation and accommodation are each occurring in sequence. Accommodation occurs as the child tries to find a way of balancing external stimuli with internal ways of organising knowledge. It is this constant but shifting balance which typifies learning and the active minds of children who are testing stimuli and trying to make sense of them.

(Edwards & Knight, 2001, p. 26)

This cycle of disequilibrium and subsequent resolution of disequilibrium is the key mechanism through which cognitive development proceeds. So cognitive development as conceptualised by Piaget involves a progressive adaptation facilitated by the ongoing interaction of concepts and the physical environment.

The adult has a responsibility to provide rich environments ... where children can ask questions, make hypotheses and form new concepts. Children have to construct learning for themselves, with the focus of learning on the reasoning processes rather than on the end products.

(French, 2007, p. 21)

Stages of thinking and understanding

Approaches to learning and development in the early years have moved beyond the constraints of a stage theory approach, as we have previously outlined. Nonetheless, it is important to acknowledge the invaluable contribution Piaget made in providing insight into very precise knowledge about how children's thinking changes and how, in turn, this advances our understanding of how children's minds develop over time. Many theorists have contributed to the body of knowledge that informs educational approaches to education in childhood, but few theorists have been able to generate the wealth and precision of detail that Piaget's theory has produced. Developmental psychologists, and Piaget in particular, have frequently been criticised for constructing an image of the child as 'deficient' by comparison with the adult (Jenks, 2005). Yet Piaget clearly saw the child's mind and way of thinking as qualitatively different to that of an adult, rather than being less able or lacking in abilities.

We have spent some time in previous chapters becoming familiar with some of the key features of each of the cognitive developmental stages that Piaget believed children's development followed. As previously outlined, when we use the term 'stage' we are referring to periods of time in which underlying mental logical structures tend to be reflected in the child's thinking and behaviour (Miller, 2010). In other words, according to Piaget, each stage has a particular structure or set of mental actions that facilitates a particular type of interaction with the world. While the senses and movement predominate in the sensorimotor period, the child moves on to the preoperational world, where symbolic representation emerges and conceptual learning becomes enabled. Within the concrete operational stage, logical thinking and the ability to carry out mental operations increases and becomes more stable in order to progress to logical and more abstract thinking and hypothetical thinking in adolescence (Young-Ihm, 2002). The importance of going beyond abstractions and generalities and being able to synthesise knowledge about how cognitive abilities emerge is summarised by Flavell (1996, p. 201) as follows:

> Piaget saw that to characterize human cognitive development adequately, one needs something less general than the functional invariants of assimilation and accommodation, co-present in all cognitive activity, but also more general than an endless list of specific acquired concepts. For Piaget, that something was cognitive structure: There has to be some tertium quid [third thing]: something which changes with age, as the functional invariants do not; but also something more general than individual contents, something which will pull diverse contents together into a single chunk.

The subtleties and complexities of Piaget's work on developmental cognitive stages have often been missed or glossed over in representations of his work based, at times, on partial readings of his very elaborate theory (Vogler *et al.*, 2008). Yet, as these authors point out, it is the simplification of Piaget's theory that has most often been drawn on to develop frameworks for early childhood education and, more broadly, developmental psychology in general. Miller suggests that despite the many amendments and certain inaccuracies that have been highlighted through post-Piagetian research, the excellent foundation of knowledge based on detailed observation of children's thinking cannot be over-estimated.

> In short, regardless of whether the various tests of Piaget's theory actually disproved some claims, the more important contribution of this burst of research energy was to contribute subtle theoretical ideas about levels of 'having' a concept and a rich set of findings about related concepts in infants and preschoolers.
>
> (2010, p. 657)

Beyond a stage theory approach to early childhood education

While stages can serve as very useful heuristics or guidelines for describing the trajectory of human behaviour, they often fail to capture the complexities of intra-individual and inter-individual variation in development. They can also place unnecessary constraints on children's learning, where a curriculum is 'pinned to age-related ways of acting in the world' (Edwards & Knight, 2001, p. 27). Young-Ihm (2002, np) reinforces these criticisms as follows:

> 'Piaget's clinical and observational studies developed the idea of readiness and explored the process by which children advance. According to this version of developmentalism, a child must be 'ready' to move on to the next developmental stage and cannot be forced to move to a higher level of cognitive functioning. Although developmentalism and readiness are widely reported to be dominant in English early childhood education, several critiques have been articulated about the readiness concept in developmentalism.

Active, child-initiated learning

Perhaps the greatest legacy of Jean Piaget to the world of early childhood education is that he challenged the existing perspectives and approaches to how a child learns. Knowledge was no longer seen as something to be transmitted passively to children, but rather was actively constructed by children themselves through hands-on and concrete experiences (Pope-Edwards, 2002). Co-construction theorists have expanded on Piaget's concept of the child as an active learner to include an emphasis on children and adults making meaning and knowledge together. While Piaget did not highlight the role of the adult in child learning, we know that interaction with and tuning in to the particular needs and abilities of the individual child makes it possible for practitioners to develop an awareness of the child's knowledge and skills and to build approaches to learning based on inter-subjectivity (Hayes, 2012).

There are many excellent illustrations in practice of how facilitating the engagement of children in hands-on and meaningful experiences can promote the active construction of knowledge. The following brief extract provides just one example of such activity. The Turtle Project was carried out in a kindergarten class at Parker Early Education Centre in Machesney Park, Illinois (Helm & Katz, 2001). The project was designed to promote understanding and knowledge around children's abilities to carry out scientific enquiry. The brief extract below is taken from documentation prepared by the teacher who recorded children's observations and comments. For several months, the children had been caring for George, a turtle who had unexpectedly turned out to be a female turtle.

What happened

The teacher brought in a log with a hole. George went into the log. George had to be awakened when it was bath time. George wasn't going to the bathroom in her tub anymore.

What we thought and said

George spends most of her time way inside the log and a little buried.
George must have been cold and wanted to get warmer.
The inside of the log was cosy and darker and warmer.

What we tried

We looked in the book about turtles that we read earlier in the year.
The children unanimously shouted 'George is hibernating!'

In this extract we see the children actively reflecting on George's change of behaviour. The teacher documents their comments and supports the children in finding out what might go towards explaining George's new behaviour pattern. Piaget's views on children's learning and development inevitably influenced the role played by those involved in children's education also – a key component of that role involved observing and guiding children to build their own knowledge rather than transmitting knowledge in a passive manner. Practitioners and teachers in early childhood education take on the roles of facilitators, models, guides and become an '*unobtrusive* director of the self-directed activity of children' (Pope-Edwards, 2002). Even the youngest of children are experts in their own learning processes when provided with opportunities to learn through hands-on and concrete experiences, as illustrated in this extract by Forman (2010, np), which documents the scientific thinking of the child in play:

> We see a 4-year-old boy standing on a board that pivots on a pipe underneath. When he stands with his weight on the right side, the board tilts all the way down to touch the ground on the right. When he shifts his weight to the left side, the board tilts all the way down to the left. We catch the action as he seeks the in-between, that is, balance. To find the in-between position, he must implement two reciprocal forces simultaneously – a little push down on the right at the same time as a little push down on the left. Earlier, he was applying only one force at a time. But these are not simply two forces, like twisting at the waist at the same time you swing a baseball bat with your arms so that you will double the distance of your hit. These forces on the pivoting board are opposing forces. The child must recognize a paradox: Together the forces do not undo each other. They yield something positive – the balance of the board.

The young child's immersion in his experience coupled with the teacher's attention to the detail of his gradual discovery and achievement of balance in this extract again provide us with an insightful illustration of the principles that Piaget promoted through his theory.

Child-motivated learning

Drawing on Piaget's legacy, contemporary models of early childhood education tend to place children at the centre of their own learning and view children as 'active authors of their own development, strongly influenced by natural, dynamic, self-righting forces within themselves, opening the way toward growth and learning' (Pope-Edwards, 2002, np). The notion of child-centred approaches to education had already been posited in previous centuries by theorists such as Rousseau, Pestalozzi and Froebel and their emphasis on the productiveness of child activity. What we have seen in many of the principles underpinning Piaget's work is a reinforcement of the notion of the child as the main driver of their own learning and acquisition of knowledge through the patterns and rules they discover in their interaction with the world around them.

Fran Paffard (2010) provides a lovely illustration of child-centred learning in practice through observing and supporting young children's schemas in play and activities. Through attentive observation of patterns of behaviour within children's play, practitioners can develop activities that follow the child's interests and build on the evidence from close observation of these patterns in order to plan for progression. The benefits of such a child-centred approach are many, including enabling practitioners to start planning from where a child is and what they can do, rather than what they cannot do (Paffard, 2010). Other benefits include respecting the child's interests, avoiding misconceptions about children's behaviours and being better able to predict the kinds of experiences that will extend a child's learning. Hayes further highlights how essential it is to build a pedagogy that places children at the centre of their learning and development:

> Such a pedagogy presumes that all minds are capable of holding ideas and beliefs: and through discussion and interaction, it can be moved towards some shared frame of reference and is child-sensitive, less patronising and more respectful of children's own role in their own development.
>
> (2012, p. xv)

Play-based curriculum

Allied to the notion of child-centred education is an understanding of the vital importance of facilitating a play-based approach to young children's learning. As we have seen throughout this book, Piaget emphasised the importance of play throughout his cognitive stages of development. From functional play in the sensorimotor period in infancy through to symbolic play and games with rules in the preoperational stages of development, learning for Piaget was enabled and supported through children's playful activities. However, Piaget did not speculate as to how play could be integrated into a pedagogy for education. Moreover, the challenges of getting beyond a limited view of play as something that is added on to rather than integrated within education have been emphasised by a number of writers in the field of early childhood education. Play, and especially dramatic play, is associated with emotional and cognitive development in that children can engage in problem-solving abilities and creativity through play (Moyles, 2010).

A lovely illustration of play-based learning approaches is provided by Brennan (2012, p. 165):

Case study: Holidays (Brennan, 2012)

Prompted by a new travel bag in the home corner, Laura and Anne play 'holidays'. They pack the bag and baby's buggy to bursting point, select magazines and proceed to the airport. Toys are purchased at the duty free shop to keep baby amused. Waving goodbye, they board the plane for Portugal. On arrival, they exude excitement and head for their hotel. The girls are very collaborative, building on one another's ideas and communicating their pleasure in each other's company.

The many gains for children's learning that can be generated through such an approach are underscored by Brennan (2012) in terms of providing opportunities for children to participate, explore, interpret and re-construct the world around them, share their ideas, knowledge and skills, and generate dialogue and reflection. It is also important to provide opportunities for practitioners to be able to share feedback on children's contributions.

Piaget's followers

Piaget has had many followers and many theorists continue to build and expand on the ideas that Piaget put forward. We have already compared the approaches of Piaget, Vygotsky and Bruner in chapter 2, with particular reference to their contributions to cognitive development in childhood. While recognising the limitations of exclusively planning early childhood education around a child's age and associated abilities, it should be acknowledged that more recent work has built on Piaget's very solid ground. Those theorists who follow in Piaget's footsteps (neo-Piagetians) define stages of development not so much in terms of their logical structure but rather in terms of the information-processing requirements that facilitate children's thinking. A good illustration of this is the development of working memory – the capacity to hold several pieces of information in mind and perform mental operations on them. Miller (2010) provides a good example of this when considering the ability to conserve volume in tall, thin glasses as opposed to short, fat glasses. Only when the child has the working memory ability to hold two conflicting representations in their mind simultaneously will they be able to integrate them to construct a new representation – taller is balanced by thinner. Other theorists heavily influenced by Piaget's theory focused on 'rule-shifts' – the development of precise rules – rather than stage-like shifts. When children have experienced an event, they develop precise rules that help them to go beyond a certain level of thought and to understand and explain a phenomenon in a more advanced way (Siegler, 1978).

How can we draw on the concepts and principles of Piaget's theory to develop a solid pedagogy for professionals working with children in the early years?

1. Learning is an active process because knowledge is constructed from within

As far as education is concerned, Kamii (1974) points out that one very strong message deriving from Piaget's theory on intellectual development is that children must be allowed to do their own learning. This statement has a consequence with regard to the teaching methodology that is implemented in the classroom. To this day, teaching is often carried out through presentation of material to be learned and by reinforcing the correct answers or outcomes that the learner gives back to the teacher. Even when an 'exploratory' or 'discovery' approach is proposed, this very often means finding out what the teacher wants the student to find out.

2. Intellectual development [learning] will be enhanced through social interaction and collaboration

Piaget was adamant that intellectual development would be enhanced through cooperation among children, but also through cooperation between the child and the teacher. The reason for this is that an interactive environment will provide opportunity for perspectives to be represented and for reflection to take place. Even conflicts between children can generate positive awareness of a particular situation or interest area.

3. The learning environment should provide opportunities for intellectual challenge and development, with a focus on actual experiences rather than language

Theorists such as Vygotsky and Bruner placed emphasis on language as a significant vehicle for learning. Piaget has been criticised for his lack of emphasis on language in learning. However, Piaget did not argue that language was not important. His argument was that language is important (Furth, 1970), but not at the expense of thinking. During the 1970s, not long after Piaget's publications, a number of theorists raised the question as to whether there exists a preoccupation at preschool level with the teaching of language at the expense of coming to terms with how the preoperational child thinks (Furth, 1970).

4. Abstract thinking will evolve from concrete actions

From an early years education point of view, this principle is very important with regards to the methodological approach the early years worker/educator chooses to implement in the classroom. If we value the notion that this principle captures, then the logical consequence must be an approach that offers opportunities for hands-on experiential learning, as opposed to more traditional approaches where the child is simply told how things work.

5. The role of the teacher is to support children in constructing their own knowledge by guiding their experiences

Piaget was convinced that 'active learning' through free exploration is the ideal way for a child to learn. The role of the adult is therefore to develop and provide, based on the curriculum, a learning environment that will provide genuine cognitive challenges with opportunities for progression for the individual children. Moreover, the role of the adult is to act as a support and a guide for the child in their learning, but also to recognise the importance of not interfering with the genuine meaning-making process that the child is engaged with.

Principles into practice

If you have read the previous issues in this series, *Introducing Vygotsky* and *Introducing Bruner* (Smidt, 2009, 2011), you will be familiar with the format where examples from practice are provided in order to illustrate the context. We have chosen to continue this approach in the hope that it will contribute to deepen your understanding of the thinking behind the theory of Piaget.

1. Learning is an active process because knowledge is constructed from within

Piaget himself made the following statement about the way that the child constructs their knowledge:

> As far as education is concerned, the chief outcome of this theory of intellectual development, is the plea that children be allowed to do their own learning . . . You cannot further understanding in a child simply by talking to him. Good pedagogy must involve presenting the child with situations in which he himself experiments, in the broadest sense of the term – trying things out to see what happens, manipulating symbols, posing questions and seeking his own answers, reconciling what he finds one time with what he finds at another, comparing his findings with those of other children . . .
>
> (Schwebel & Raph, 1974, p. 2)

The above statement sets Piaget's pedagogical approach apart from traditional teaching practice, where the teacher presents the child with material to be learned and where a particular outcome is expected.

Case study 1

In a toddler room in a crèche, as a part of their current focus on cold climate animals, the early years educator has decided that the children should learn about penguins, so she wants them to carry out an art activity where they will create their own penguin face. In preparation for this activity, she has carefully selected the materials to be used by the children; a paper plate which makes up the shape of the face, some triangles for a beak, which she has cut out from orange cardboard, a bag of plastic wiggle eyes, a tube of glue and black and white paint.

In order to help the child to understand what to do, she has made a template, which she will show to the children before they start. As she understands the challenges of working with a large group of children, she has decided to work with small groups, so a maximum of three children will be allowed at the table at any given time. If one child completes her penguin, another child will be called to join the activity until all children have completed the task.

If we stop to reflect on the example above, we can identify a number of issues that contradict Piaget's view that the child is an active learner and that learning takes place through self-directed activity. Let's explore the reasons why.

Although the activity offers the opportunity for the child to act upon the materials, the genuine sense of exploration and discovery has been severely hampered by the fact that the teacher has set the parameters for the activity and thereby restricted the children's possibilities of creating the penguin as they understand it. Furthermore, as the product outcomes are so predictive, it deprives the child of the opportunity to compare and contrast with what other children choose to do when carrying out the task. Another problem with this scenario is that the children do not choose to do the activity themselves, but are led into it by the adult. The adult chose the activity and the outcomes and therefore it does not represent a genuine learning opportunity.

So, how could the teacher present this activity differently? A number of great learning opportunities present themselves from the outset of this activity: opportunities for discussing the project together, deciding what materials are suitable, deciding what to do with the product. The activity should also be carried out at a time when the child has the motivation to carry it out, rather than at a time when the adult decides that the time is right. In the context of a Piagetian approach, the learning would be diminished by the fact that the children would be asked to end one activity in order to start another.

2. Intellectual development [learning] will be enhanced through social interaction and collaboration

When discussing the role of socio-cultural factors in intellectual development, early years educators and researchers often turn to Vygotsky, particularly with regards to the importance of language. Likewise, Piaget is often criticised for not placing a strong enough emphasis on the importance of these two factors, and popular thought is that the Piagetian child is a lone scientist where knowledge is constructed outside of a social context and social factors are not foregrounded. However, Piaget's theory provides an opportunity to extend on Vygotsky's approach to how the child develops intellectually. For example, Piaget argues that children cannot by themselves establish consistency in their use of symbols (such as language or numbers) if they are left to play on their own, and that language will work to further develop the links between schemas. So, as the child interacts with others socially, language will contribute to enable schemas to interact with each other and to allow the extension of schemas to higher levels.

This interactive environment described in Case study 2 provides a wonderful framework for the children to apply themselves intellectually and is an example of how social interaction and collaboration can become a vehicle for cognitive development.

Case study 2

Anna and Ali are playing together on the computer in the preschool classroom. On the screen is a game called Big and Small House and the objective of the game is to make decisions related to the size of different objects as they wander around in a house. The girls are discussing the possible options loudly, giving instructions and providing feedback to each other based on the decisions they made.

One of the characters in the game is called 'Small' and he loves bouncing on his bed. The girls have to help calm him down by finding things in the room that will have a calming effect on him. Ali suggests that Anna gives him a pillow and points at it. But Anna argues that there is a smaller pillow in the room and that this must belong to Small, as it is smaller than the other, and the bigger one must belong to Big.

---

3. The learning environment should provide opportunity for intellectual challenge and development, with a focus on actual experiences rather than language

In a Piagetian classroom the presentation of ready-made knowledge is de-emphasised, and children are encouraged to discover for themselves through spontaneous interaction with the environment. Therefore, instead of teaching didactically, teachers provide a rich variety of activities that permit children to act directly on the physical world. In order to provide a context for this idea, we could turn to the following story, as told by a French educator, Alain:

> A man on a train is 'reading' the newspaper. And when the man sitting next to him asks 'What is in the news today?', he replies 'I don't know, I'm just reading!'

As mentioned in the introduction to this book (p. vii), Piaget took an interest in the work of another French educationalist, Célestin Freinet, who thought the above quote a mind-deadening technique. Reading, according to Freinet, should be a search for meaning, not perceived synthetically, letter by letter, but globally, similar to the 'Whole language' method that teaches children how to read by beginning with complete words. Freinet introduced a printing press in the school, so that the children could be encouraged to read because this would be required of them in order to do their job well, so they would in essence have a vested interest in mastering these skills. Taking this approach into the early years classroom, the children should be able to access learning material that would be very much hands-on, such as the sand and water table where, through play, children are encouraged to experiment and where it is easy for the teacher to set and guide learning outcomes.

Case study 3

Like most other children, Claire (age 4) likes to spend time at the sand table. She digs, sifts, builds, pours and she enjoys the feel and smell of it, pretends with it and explores how it moves. There is no right way to use sand, it invites participation; it permits children to make and test hypotheses; it stretches the imagination; it provides a potentially soothing, sensory experience; and it is an excellent avenue for children to learn physical, cognitive and social skills. Because sand play is open-ended, the child determines the direction and path of his or her own play. This freedom then clears the way for the child to build developmental concepts in a way that is entirely meaning-making to the individual child.

So, a sand table, or a sand pit, fits really nicely with Piaget's idea that children have an inner drive to understand the world that surrounds them. Concepts about how the world works are built gradually and become increasingly complex as the child enters a rich learning environment and exercises his or her freedom to play.

4. Abstract thinking will evolve from concrete actions

In an early education context, educators have long realised that a direct, traditional teaching method is not suitable for young children. They understand that it is necessary for a child to have concrete experiences in

---

Case study 4

For his 6th birthday, Charlie received a transistor radio/cassette player as a present from his parents. Being of a curious nature and very nimble with his fingers, he soon started to take it apart to see what it looked like inside. It may not have been an example to follow, for health and safety reasons. But a few weeks later, when he accidentally dropped it on the ground and it broke, he could fairly accurately pinpoint what the damage was and furthermore, he was able to communicate to his father what he thought the issues were. Through acting on the object (the radio), and because he had learned how it works, Charlie was now able to relate abstractly to the situation in the discussion.

order to fully understand how an object functions. Kamii (1974) describes concrete experience as referring to direct contact and with real objects and events, whereas abstract thinking refers to the use of representation and the so-called higher order concepts. If the child can spend time manipulating an object, they will naturally understand more of how the object works.

5. The role of the teacher is to support children in constructing their own knowledge by guiding their experiences

Coming from a constructivist viewpoint, the educator's role in the Piagetian school is to structure a rich environment, observe what children are doing and thinking and avoid interactions that will take away from the genuine experience of the child. Instead, the teacher should 'encourage problem solving, perspective taking, and/or consideration of feelings' (Chaille & Britain, 1997, p. 65). Open-ended play can be fostered by using open-ended questions such as:

- How could you fix that?
- What else could you do?
- What would happen if you . . .?
- What do you think/feel about . . .?
- How did you do that?
- How could you do that in a different way?

By asking open-ended questions, the teacher provides an environment that enables the child to learn more than they could on their own. Vygotsky referred to this as the 'zone of proximal development' (Smidt, 2009) and Piaget's ideal teacher works in a very similar fashion.

Case study 5

Amanda (age 5) has chosen to make a painting using water colours, and Nicky, her key worker, is sitting down at the table directly opposite her. Amanda starts by mixing some colours and Nicky is interested in knowing what she has decided to do. 'What do you think?', says Nicky. 'I am making light pink', answers Amanda. 'I can see that you are mixing white and red', Nicky confirms, trying to name what Amanda has done, but being careful not to control what Amanda is doing. 'I want to paint a tree', Amanda exclaims. 'OK, what colours do you need for the tree?', asks Nicky. Amanda answers, 'It will be a pink tree, with red leaves'. She continues, 'You see, a red squirrel lives in the tree and I think it will like red leaves, because nobody can see it if it sits in the branches.' That's a great idea', praises Nicky. 'I notice a little yellow in there, what are you using that for?' asks Nicky. 'I haven't decided yet', says Amanda. 'Maybe I will make it into pink?' She proceeds to put red in with the yellow. 'What happened now?', asks Nicky. 'It is a different kind of pink', says Amanda. 'What colours did you put together?', asks Nicky. Amanda confirms that it was yellow and red. 'What kind of colour did you get?', Nicky continues. 'It is orange!', Amanda shouts out. 'It is orange pink!'

Observing and documenting children's learning

We conclude our journey through Piaget's stages of development reflecting on perhaps the greatest of his legacies for educators in early childhood – his passion for detail and his wonderful attention to the minutiae of children's minds as they develop from infancy into adolescence. Among the many principles that his theory has generated, a simple yet powerful message that comes across is the profound importance of observing and documenting children as they act upon their worlds. Forman and Hall (2005, np) capture the value of 'wondering with children' in the following extract:

> Considering children's theories requires more than a careful transcription of what they say and do. We have to dig. We have to abstract the meaning of elliptical sentences, aborted movements, or a confusing explanation, request, or description. Children are competent learners, but as teachers, we have to slow down, carefully observe, and study our documented observations in order to understand the ideas that they are attempting to convey. In addition to slowing down, observing, and studying children's actions and narration, understanding children's theories requires a general knowledge of child development and a willingness to speculate.

Glossary

Accommodation   A part of the process of adaptation. When learning new information, humans may change their understanding of an idea to incorporate the new information into their previous understanding of an idea. For example, a child may learn that 'food is good'. Later, he/she may taste food he does not like. His understanding of food would then change to 'some food is good, and some tastes bad'.

Active learning   The idea of the child being very curious and doing everything possible to understand the world.

Adaptation   Piaget's term for what most of us would call learning, referring to the ability to adjust to new information and experiences. Learning is essentially adapting to our constantly changing environment. Through adaptation, we are able to adopt new behaviours that allow us to cope with change.

Assimilation   Another part of the process of adaptation. Through assimilation, we take in new information or experiences and incorporate them into our existing ideas. The process is somewhat subjective, because we tend to modify experience or information somewhat to fit in with our pre-existing beliefs.

Centration   A limitation of preoperational thought that leads the child to focus on one aspect of a situation and neglect others, often leading to illogical conclusions.

Cognitive development   The development of thinking and reasoning, solving problems, communicating ideas. Also called intellectual or mental development.

Concrete operational stage   The third stage of cognitive development (approximately from ages 7 to 12), during which children develop logical but not abstract thinking.

Conservation   Awareness that two objects that are equal according to a certain measure (such as length, weight or quantity) remain equal in the face of perceptual alteration (for example, a change in shape or volume) so long as nothing has been added to or taken away from either object.

Equilibration   Piaget believed that all children try to strike a balance between assimilation and accommodation, which is achieved through a mechanism Piaget called equilibration. As children progress through the stages of cognitive development, it is important to maintain a balance between applying previous knowledge (assimilation) and changing behaviour to account for new knowledge (accommodation). Equilibration helps explain how children are able to move from one stage of thought into the next.

Exploration   The process of being an active learner by exploring everything in order to find out more. Synonymous with investigation or discovery.

Formal operational stage   The fourth and final stage of cognitive development, characterised by the ability to think abstractly.

Irreversibility   A limitation on preoperational thought, consisting of failure to understand that an operation can go in two or more directions.

Object permanence   The understanding that a person or an object still exists when out of sight.

Organisation   Integration of knowledge into a system to make sense of the environment.

Preoperational stage   The second stage of cognitive development (approximately from ages 2 to 7), in which children become more sophisticated in their use of symbolic thought but are not yet able to use logic.

Reflection   Often means 'thinking about' and develops along with the person's ability to think abstractly.

Representational ability   Capacity to mentally represent objects and experiences, largely through the use of symbols.

Schemas   A schema describes both the mental and physical actions involved in understanding and knowing. Schemas are categories of knowledge that help us to interpret and understand the world.

Sensorimotor stage   The first stage of cognitive development, during which infants (from birth to approximately 2 years) learn through their developing senses and motor activities.

Symbolic function   Ability to use mental representations (words, numbers or images) to which a child has attached meaning; this ability, characteristic of preoperational thought, is shown in deferred imitation, symbolic play and language.

Transduction   A preoperational child's tendency to mentally link particular experiences, whether or not there is logically a causal relationship.

References

Ackermann, E. (1996). Perspective taking and object construction. In Y. R. Kafai & M. Resnick (eds), *Constructionism in Practice* (pp. 25–37). Mahwah, NJ: Lawrence Erlbaum Associates.

Ackermann, E. (2001). Piaget's Constructivism, Papert's Constructivism: What's the difference? Available at: http://learning.media.mit.edu/content/publications/ EA.Piaget%20_%20Papert.pdf

Allery, G. (2010). Observing symbolic play. In Smidt, S. (ed.), *Key Issues in Early Years Education* (pp. 35–36). London: Routledge.

Arnold, C. (1999). *Child Development and Learning 2–5 Years: Georgia's Story.* London: Paul Chapman.

Arnold, C. (2003). *Observing Harry: Child Development and Learning 0–5.* Maidenhead: Open University Press.

Arnold, C. (2010). *Understanding Schemas and Emotion in Early Childhood.* London: Sage.

Athey, C. (1990). *Extending Thought in Young Children: A Parent–Teacher Partnership.* London: Paul Chapman.

Baillargeon, R., Li, J., Gertner, Y., & Wu, D. (2011). How do infants reason about physical events. In U. Goswami (ed.), *The Wiley-Blackwell Handbook of Childhood Cognitive Development* (pp. 11–48). Oxford: Wiley-Blackwell.

Bancroft, D., & Flynn, E. (2005). Early cognitive development. In J. Oates, C. Wood, & A. Grayson (eds), *Psychological Development in the Early Years* (pp. 131–167). Milton Keynes: Blackwell Publishing in association with The Open University.

Baron-Cohen, S. (2001). Theory of mind in normal development and autism. *Prisme, 34,* 174–183.

Bartsch, K., & Wellman, H. M. (1995). *Children Talk About the Mind.* Oxford: Oxford University Press.

Bell, S. M. (1970). The development of the concept of object as related to infant-mother attachment. *Child Development, 41*(2), 292–311.

Bergen, D. (2002). The role of pretend play in children's cognitive development. *Early Childhood: Research and Practice, 4* [online]. Available at: http://ecrp.uiuc. edu/v4n1/bergen.html.

Blakemore, S., & Frith, U. (2005). *The Learning Brain: Lessons for Education.* Oxford: Blackwell.

Bower, T., Broughton, J., & Moore, M. (1971). Development of the object concept as manifested in the tracking behaviour of infants between 7 and 20 weeks of age. *Journal of Experimental Psychology,* 11, 182–193.

Bradford, H. (2012). *Appropriate Environments for Children Under Three*. London: Routledge.

Brennan, C. (ed.) (2004). *The Power of Play: A Play Curriculum in Action*. Dublin: IPPA.

Brennan, C. (2012). Learning to play and playing to learn. In M. Mhic Mhathuna & M. Taylor (eds), *Early Childhood Education and Care: An Introduction for Students in Ireland* (pp. 161–167). Dublin: Gill & Macmillan.

Brewer, R. A. (2010). The Canada Goose Project: a first project with children under 3. *Early Childhood Research and Practice*, *12*(1) [online]. Available at: http://ecrp.uiuc.edu/v12n1/brewer.html.

Bruner, J. S. (1976). Prelinguistic prerequisites of speech. In R. Campbell & P. Smith (eds), *Recent Advances in the Psychology of Language* (pp. 199–214). New York: Plenum Press.

Chaille, C., & Britain, L. (1997). *The Young Child as Scientist*. New York: Longman.

Cook, J. L., & Cook, C. (2008). *Child Development: Principles and Perspectives* (2nd edn). New York: Pearson.

DeHart, G., Sroufe, A., & Cooper, R. (2004). *Child Development: Its Nature and Course* (5th edn). New York: McGraw-Hill.

DeMarie, D. (2001). A trip to the zoo: children's words and photographs. *Early Childhood Research and Practice*, *3*(1) [online]. Available at: http://ecrp.uiuc.edu/v3n1/demarie.html.

De Waal, F. B. (2008). Putting the altruism back in altruism: the evolution of empathy. *Annual Review of Psychology*, 59, 279–300.

Diamond, A. (1985). Development of the ability to use recall to guide action as indicated by infants' performance on A-not-B. *Child Development*, *56*, 868–883.

Diamond, A. (2000). Close interrelation of motor development and cognitive development and of the cerebullum and prefrontal cortex. *Child Development*, *71*, 44–56.

Donaldson, M. (1978). *Children's Minds*. London: Taylor & Francis.

Drummond, M. J. (2010). Under the microscope. In S. Smidt (ed.), *Key Issues in Early Years Education* (pp. 37–44). Oxford: Routledge.

Edwards, A., & Knight, P. (2001). *Effective Early Years Education*. Milton Keynes: Open University Press.

Eisenberg, N., Shea, C. L., Carlo, G., & Knight, G. (1991). Empathy-related responding and cognition: a 'chicken and the egg' dilemma. In W. K. J. Gewirtz (ed.), *Handbook of Moral Behavior and Development:* (Vol. 2, pp. 63–88). Hillsdale, NJ: Erlbaum.

Elkind, D. (1967). Egocentrism in adolescence. *Child Development*, *38*(4), 1025–1034.

Fabian, H., & Dunlop, A. W. (2007). *Informing Transitions in the Early Years: Research, Policy & Practice*. Maidenhead: Open University Press.

Fisher, K., & Bullock, D. (1984). Cognitive development in school age children: conclusions and new directions. In W. A. Collins (ed.), *Development During Middle Childhood: The Years from Six to Twelve* (pp. 70–146). Washington, DC: National Academy Press.

Flavell, J. (1963). *The Developmental Psychology of Jean Piaget*. Princeton, NJ: D. Van Nostrand.

Flavell, J. (1990). Perspectives on perspective-taking. Paper presented at the 20th Annual Symposium of the Jean Piaget Society. Philadelphia, June 2.

Flavell, J. (1996). Piaget's legacy. *Psychological Science, 7*, 200–203.

Forman, G. (2010). When 2-year-olds and 3-year-olds think like scientists. *Early Childhood Research and Practice, 12*(2) [online]. Available at: http://ecrp.uiuc.edu/v12n2/forman.html.

Forman, G., & Hall, E. (2005). Wondering with children: the importance of observation in early education. *Early Childhood Research and Practice, 7*(2) [online]. Available at: http://ecrp.uiuc.edu/v7n2/forman.html.

French, G. (2007). The Framework for Early Learning: A Background Paper. Children's Early Learning and Development. Dublin: National Council for Curriculum and Assessment.

Furth, H. G. (1970). *Piaget for Teachers*. Englewood Cliffs, NJ: Prentice-Hall.

Geangu, E. (2009). Empathy development – insights from early years. An introduction to the special issue. *Cognition, Brain & Behaviour: An Interdisciplinary Journal, 13*, 363–366.

Gelman, R. (1972). The nature and development of early number concepts. *Advanced Child Development, 7*, 115–167.

Ginsburg, H. P., Klein, A., & Starkey, P. (1998). The development of children's mathematical thinking: connecting research with practice. In W. Damon, R. M. Lerner, K. A. Renninger, & I. E. Sigel (eds), *Handbook of Child Psychology: Child Psychology in Practice* (Vol. 4, pp. 401–476). New York: Wiley.

Gopnik, A. (2010). How babies think. *Scientific American, 303*, 76–81.

Gopnik, A. (2012). Causality. In P. Zelazo (ed.), *The Oxford Handbook of Developmental Psychology* (pp. 628–649). New York: Oxford University Press

Gopnik, A., Meltzoff, A., & Kuhl, P. (2001). *The Scientist in the Crib: What Early Learning Tells Us About the Mind*. New York: Harper Perennial.

Goswami, U. (2011). Inductive and deductive reasoning. In U. Goswami (ed.), *The Wiley-Blackwell Handbook of Cognitive Development in Childhood* (pp. 399–419). Oxford: Blackwell.

Halford, G., & Andrews, G. (2011). Information-processing models of cognitive development. In U. Goswami (ed.), *The Wiley-Blackwell Handbook of Cognitive Development in Childhood* (pp. 697–719). Oxford: Blackwell.

Hayes, N. (2012). Introduction: children at the centre of practice. In M. MhicMhathuna & M. Taylor (eds), *Early Childhood Education & Care* (pp. xi–xviii). Dublin: Gill & McMillan.

Helm, J., & Katz, L. (2001). *Young Investigators: The Project Approach in the Early Years*. New York: Teachers College Press.

Hetherington, E. M., & Parke, R. (2003). *Child Psychology: A Contemporary Viewpoint*. New York: McGraw-Hill.

Hirsh-Pasek, K., Golinkoff, R., Berk, L., & Singer, D. (2009). *A Mandate for Playful Learning in Preschool: Presenting the Evidence*. New York: Oxford University Press.

Hughes, B. (2003). Play deprivation, play bias and playwork practice. In F. Brown (ed.), *Playwork Theory and Practice* (pp. 66–80). Maidenhead: Open University Press.

Hyson, M., Biggar Tomlinson, H., & Morris, C. (2009). Quality improvement in early childhood teacher education: faculty perspectives and recommendations for the future. *Early Childhood Research and Practice, 14*(1) [online]. Available at http://ecrp.uiuc.edu/v11n1/hyson.html

Inhelder, B., & Piaget, J. (1958). *The Growth of Logical Thinking from Childhood to Adolescence*. New York: Basic Books.

Inhelder, B., & Piaget, J. (1964). *The Early Growth of Logic in the Child*. London: Routledge & Kegan Paul.

Jenks, C. (2005). *Childhood*. Abingdon: Routledge.

Kamii, C. (1974). Pedagogical priciples derived from Piaget's theory: relevance for educational practice. In M. R. Schwebel & J. Raph (eds), *Piaget in the Classroom* (pp. 199–214). London: Routledge & Kegan Paul.

Kavanaugh, R. D. (2006). Pretend play and theory of mind. In L. Balter & C. S. Tamis-LeMonda (eds), *Child Psychology: A Handbook of Contemporary Issues* (pp. 153–166). New York: Psychology Press.

Kirova, A., & Bhargava, A. (2002). Learning to guide preschool children's mathematical understanding: a teacher's professional growth. *Early Childhood Research and Practice*, 4(1) [online]. Available at http://ecrp.uiuc.edu/v4n1/kirova.html

Knafo, A., Zahn-Waxler, C., Van Hulle, C., Robinson, J. L., & Rhee, S. H. (2008). The developmental origins of a disposition toward empathy: genetic and environmental contributions. *Emotions*, *8*, 737–752.

Krogh, S., & Slentz, K. (2001). *The Early Childhood Curriculum*. Mawah, NJ: Lawrence Erlbaum.

Labinowicz, E. (1985). *Learning from Children: New Beginnings for Teaching Numerical Thinking*. Menlo Park, CA: Addison-Wesley.

Lillard, A., Lerner, M., Hopkins, E., Dore, R., Smith, E., & Palmquis, C. (2012). The impact of pretend play on children's development: a review of the evidence. *Psychological Bulletin*, *139*, 1–34 doi: 10.1037/a0029321.

May, P. (2011). *Child Development in Practice: Responsive Teaching and Learning from Birth to Five*. New York: Routledge.

McGarrigle, J., & Donaldson, M. (1974). Conservation accidents. *Cognition*, *3*, 341–350.

Meadows, S. (1993). *The Child as Thinker: The Development and Acquisition of Cognition in Childhood*. Hove: Routledge.

Meltzoff, A., & Moore, M. (1994). Imitation, memory, and the representation of persons. *Infant Behavior and Development*, *17*, 83–99.

Meltzoff, A. N., Gopnik, A., & Repacholi, B. M. (1999). Toddlers' understanding of intentions, desires, and emotions: explorations of the dark ages. In P. D. Zelazo, J. W. Astington, & D. R. Olson (eds), *Developing Theories of Intention: Social Understanding and Self Control* (pp. 17–41). Mahwah, NJ: Lawrence Erlbaum.

Miller, P. H. (1990). The development of strategies of selective attention. In D. F. Bjorklund (ed.), *Children's Strategies: Contemporary Views of Cognitive Development* (pp. 157–184). Hillsdale, NJ: Erlbaum.

Miller, P. (2011). Piaget's theory: past, present, and future. In U. Goswami (ed.), *The Wiley-Blackwell Handbook of Cognitive Development in Childhood* (pp. 649–672). Oxford: Blackwell.

Miller, S. (2010). Social-cognitive development in early childhood. In B. R. Tremblay, M. Boivin, & R. DeV. Peters (eds), *Encyclopedia on Early Childhood Development [online]* (pp. 1–5). Montreal: Montreal Centre of Excellence for Early Childhood Development.

Moyles, J. (2010). Play: the powerful means of learning in the early years. In S. Smidt (ed.), *Key Issues in Early Years Education* (pp. 23–33). London: Routledge.

NCCA (2009). *Aistear: the Early Childhood Curriculum Framework*. Dublin: National Council for Curriculum Assessment.

Oates, J., Sheehy, K., & Wood, C. (2005). Theories of development. In J. Oates, C. Wood, & A. Grayson (eds), *Psychological Development and Early Childhood* (pp. 49–87). Milton Keynes: Blackwell Publishing in association with The Open University.

Opfer, J., & Gelman, S. (2011). Development of the animate–inanimate distinction. In U. Goswami (ed.), *The Wiley-Blackwell Handbook of Cognitive Development in Childhood* (pp. 213–238). Oxford: Blackwell.

Oswalt, A. (2010). *Cognitive development: Piaget's concrete operations*. Available at: http://www.mentalhelp.net/poc/view_doc.php?type=doc&id=37677&cn=1272.

Paffard, F. (2010). Patterns of play: observing and supporting young children's schemas. In S. Smidt (ed.), *Key Issues in Early Years Education* (pp. 48–56). London: Routledge.

Parke, R., & Gauvain, M. (2008). *Child Psychology: A Contemporary Viewpoint*. New York: McGraw-Hill.

Perner, J., Leekam, S. R., & Wimmer, H. (1987). Three-year-olds' difficulty with false belief: the case for a conceptual deficit. *British Journal of Developmental Psychology*, 5, 125–137.

Phillips, J. (1969). *The Origins of Intellect: Piaget's Theory*. Michigan: W. H. Freeman.

Phillips, S., Wilson, W. H., & Halford, G. S. (2009). What do transitive inference and class inclusion have in common? Categorical (co)products and cognitive development. *PLOS Computational Biology*, 5(12), e1000599. doi:10.1371/journal.pcbi.1000599.

Piaget, J. (1929). *The Child's Conception of the World*. New York: Harcourt Brace Javanovich.

Piaget, J. (1930/1969). *The Child's Conception of Physical Causality*. Totowa, NJ: Litttlefield, Adams.

Piaget, J. (1932). *The Moral Judgement of the Child*. New York: Free Press.

Piaget, J. (1951). *Play, Dreams and Imagination in Childhood*. London: Heinemann in association with the New Education Fellowship.

Piaget, J. (1952). *The Origins of Intelligence in Children*. New York: Norton.

Piaget, J. (1954). *The Construction of Reality in the Child* (M. Cook, Trans.). New York: Basic Books.

Piaget, J. (1955). *The Construction of Reality in the Child*. London: Routledge & Kegan Paul.

Piaget, J. (1959). *The Language and Thought of the Child*. London: Routledge & Kegan Paul.

Piaget, J. (1960). *The Child's Conception of the World*. London: Routledge.

Piaget, J. (1962). *Play, Dreams and Imitation in Childhood*. New York: Norton.

Piaget, J. & Inhelder, B. (1956). *The Child's Conception of Space*. London: Routledge & Kegan Paul.

Pope-Edwards, C. (2002). Three approaches from Europe: Waldorf, Montessori, and Reggio Emilia. *Early Childhood Research and Practice*, 4(1) [online]. Available at: http://ecrp.uiuc.edu/v4n1/edwards.html.

Price-Williams, D., Gordon, W., & Ramirez, M. (1969). Skill and conservation: a study of pottery-making children. *Developmental Psychology, 1*, 769.

PsyBlog: Understand Your Mind. (2008) *Infants are Intuitive Physicists: Object Permanence* [online]. Available at: http://www.spring.org.uk/2008/06/infants-are-intuitive-physicists-object.php

Rizzolatti, G., & Craighero, L. (2004). The mirror-neuron system. *Annual Review of Neuroscience, 27*, 169–192.

Robinson, M. (2011). *Understanding Behaviour and Development in Early Childhood.* London: Routledge.

Robson, S., & Hargreaves, D. (2005). What do early childhood practitioners think about young children's thinking? *European Early Childhood Education Research Journal, 13*(1), 81–96.

Rosengren, K., & Hickling, A. (2000). Metamorphosis and magic: the development of children's thinking about possible events and plausible mechanisms. In K. Rosengren, C. Johnson, & P. Harris (eds), *Imagining the Impossible: Magical, Scientific and Religious Thinking in Children* (pp. 75–98). New York: Cambridge University Press.

Santrock, J. (2011). *Child Development* (13th edn). New York: McGraw-Hill.

Schaffer, R. (2006). *Key Concepts in Developmental Psychology* (2nd edn). London: Sage.

Schwebel, M., & Raph, J. (1974). *Piaget in the Classroom.* London: Routledge & Kegan Paul.

Shayer, M., & Wylam, H. (1978). The distribution of Piagetian stages of thinking in British middle and secondary school children. *British Journal of Educational Psychology, 48*, 62–70.

Siegler, R. S. (1978). The origins of scientific reasoning. In R. S. Siegler (ed.), *Children's Thinking: What Develops?* (pp. 109–149). Hillsdale, NJ: Erlbaum.

Siegler, R. S. (1991). *Children's Thinking* (2nd edn). Englewood Cliffs, NJ: Prentice-Hall.

Slaughter, V., & Boh, W. (2001). Decalage in infants' search for mothers versus toys demonstrated with a delayed response task. *Infancy, 2*, 405–413.

Smidt, S. (2009). *Introducing Vygotsky: A Guide for Practitioners in Early Years Education.* London: Routledge.

Smidt, S. (ed.) (2010). *Key Issues in the Early Years.* London: Routledge.

Smidt, S. (2011). *Introducing Bruner: A Guide for Practitioners and Students in Early Years Education.* London: Routledge.

Smith, P., Cowie, H., & Blades, M. (2003). *Understanding Children's Development* (4th edn). Oxford: Blackwell.

Spencer, C., & Hall, E. (2010). Dramatic play as a context for children's investigation of size and scale. *Early Childhood Research and Practice, 12*(2) [online]. Available at http://ecrp.uiuc.edu/v12n2/spencer.html

Stafford, P. (2012). Numeracy through play and real-life experiences. In M. M. Mhathuna & M. Taylor (eds), *Early Childhood Education and Care: An Introduction for Students in Ireland* (pp. 241–253). Dublin: Gill & Macmillan.

Sylva, K., Melhuish, E., Sammons, P., Siram-Blatchford, I., & Taggart, B. (2004). *The Effective Provision of Pre-School Education (EPPE) Project: Findings from the Early Primary Years.* Nottingham: Department for Education Publications.

Tassoni, P. (2012). *Practical EYFS Handbook.* London: Pearson.

Thornton, S. (2002). *Growing Minds*. Basingstoke: Palgrave Macmillan.

Van der Mark, I. L., Van IJzendoorn, M. H., & Bakermans-Kranenburg, M. J. (2002). Development of empathy in girls during the second year of life: associations with parenting, attachment, and temperament. *Social Development*, *11*(4), 451–468.

Van Meeteren, B., & Zan, B. (2010). 'Revealing the work of young engineers in early childhood education'. Paper presented at the SEED (STEM in Early Education and Development) Conference. Early Childhood Research and Practice. Available at: http://ecrp.uiuc.edu/beyond/seed/zan.html.

Vogler, P., Crivello, G., & Woodhead, M. (2008). Early childhood transitions research: a review of concepts, theory, and practice. Working Paper No. 48. Bernard van Leer Foundation.

Vygotsky, L. (1967). Play and its role in the mental development of the child. *Soviet Psychology*, *5*, 6–18.

Vygotsky, L. (1986). *Thought and Language*. Cambridge, MA: MIT Press.

Wallace, B. (2002). *Teaching Thinking Skills Across the Early Years*. London: David Fulton.

Warneken, F., & Tomasello, M. (2007). Helping and cooperation at 14 months of age. *Infancy*, *11*, 271–294.

Wellman, H., & Gelman, S. (1998). Knowledge acquisition in foundational domains. In W. Damon, D. Kuhn, & R. Siegler (eds), *Handbook of Child Psychology: Vol. 2. Cognition, Language, and Perception* (5th edn, pp. 523–574). New York: Wiley.

White, J. (2002). *The Child's Mind*. London: Routledge/Falmer.

Whitebread, D. (2012). *Developmental Psychology & Early Childhood Education*. London: Sage.

Willatts, P. (1989). Development of problem solving in infancy. In A. Slater & J. G. Bremner (eds.), *Infant Development* (143–182). Hove: Lawrence Erlbaum.

Wood, D. (ed.) (1998). *How Children Think and Learn*. Oxford: Blackwell Press.

Wood, E., & Atfield, J. (2005). *Play, Learning and the Early Childhood Curriculum* (2nd edn). London: Sage.

Young-Ihm, K. (2002). Changing curriculum for early childhood education in England. *Early Childhood Research and Practice*, *4*(2) [online]. Available at http://ecrp.uiuc.edu/v4n2/kwon.html.

Zelazo, P. D., Reznick, J. S., & Piñon, D. E. (1995). Response control and the execution of verbal rules. *Developmental Psychology*, *31*, 508–517.

Index

Page references in *italics* indicate a figure and those in **bold** a table.